A Practical Guide to Fashion Law and Compliance

A Practical Guide to Fashion Law and Compliance

Deanna Clark-Esposito

FAIRCHILD BOOKS

NEW YORK • LONDON • OXFORD • NEW DELHI • SYDNEY

FAIRCHILD BOOKS
Bloomsbury Publishing Inc
1385 Broadway, New York, NY 10018, USA

BLOOMSBURY, FAIRCHILD BOOKS and the Fairchild Books logo are trademarks of
Bloomsbury Publishing Plc

This edition first published 2018

Cover design by Alice Marwick

Bloomsbury Publishing Inc does not have any control over, or responsibility for, any
third-party websites referred to or in this book. All internet addresses given in this book
were correct at the time of going to press. The author and publisher regret any
inconvenience caused if addresses have changed or sites have ceased to exist, but can
accept no responsibility for any such changes.

Library of Congress Cataloging-in-Publication Data
Names: Clark-Esposito, Deanna, author.
Title: A practical guide to fashion law and compliance / Deanna Clark-Esposito, Fashion
    Institute of Technology, New York.
Description: New York : Fairchild Books, an imprint of Bloomsbury Publishing Inc, 2018. |
    Includes index.
Identifiers: LCCN 2017040432 | ISBN 9781501322891 (pbk.)
Subjects: LCSH: Clothing trade–Law and legislation–United States.
Classification: LCC KF3409.C56 C57 2018 | DDC 344.7304/235–dc23 LC record available
    at https://lccn.loc.gov/2017040432

ISBN: PB: 978-1-5013-2289-1
         ePDF: 978-1-5013-2290-7

Typeset by RefineCatch Limited, Bungay, Suffolk
Printed and bound in the United States of America

To find out more about our authors and books visit www.fairchildbooks.com and sign up for
our newsletters.

Contents

List of illustrations

List of boxes and table

Boxes

Table

Acknowledgments

I would like to extend a warm heartfelt "thank you" to all of the following people, for whom without their support in writing this text, the book would not have been possible. First, to those presently and formerly of Bloomsbury Publishing for helping me navigate the publishing process, I thank Joe Miranda, Edie Weinberg, Amanda Breccia, Colette Meacher, and Priscilla McGeehon, as well as the peer reviewers who helped me take the draft manuscript and make it even stronger. To my contributors for lending your wisdom to the text with your first-hand knowledge about the industry, I thank Frances Corner, Bill D'Arienzo, Nimet Degirmencioglu, Amy DuFault, Kristin Grant, Shanley Knox, Anthony Lilore, Jasmin Malik Chua, Laurie Marshall, Timo Rissanen, Chad Schofield, Adam Varley, and Irving Williamson. To those who leant their tips and strategies for writing the text, I thank Kate Black, Susie Breuer, Robert Clougherty, Jacqui Jenkins, Gordon Kendall, Christine Pomeranz, Jennifer Prendergast, Janis Salek, Bill Shayne, Francesca Sterlacci, and Dorcas Tominaga. Last but not least, I would like to thank my husband Gennaro Esposito, for his patience, kindness, and amazing cooking and music throughout this process.

About the author

Deanna is the Managing Attorney of the Clark-Esposito Law Firm, P.C. in New York City covering fashion, international trade, transportation, and other legal matters. She is an Executive Member of Fashion Group International (NY) and the President of the New York chapter of the Organization of Women in International Trade. She teaches at the Fashion Institute of Technology and is an avid presenter with several organizations including, the US Small Business Administration. Deanna is a native of San Francisco and resides in New York City. More information on her may be found at www.clarkespositolaw.com.

Disclaimer

The following materials are for instructional purposes only. Nothing herein constitutes, is intended to constitute, or should be relied on as legal advice or as creating an attorney–client relationship with the author. The author and Bloomsbury Publishing expressly disclaim any responsibility for any direct or consequential damages related in any way to anything contained in the material, which are provided on an "as-is" basis, and any real-life application of the materials in this text should be independently verified in advance of use by experienced counsel.

Words in **bold** throughout the text are described in the Glossary at the end of the book.

Preface

A book for "the people"

Five years ago when I first put pen to paper and began sketching out this book, its purpose was twofold. First, I wanted to create a book "for the people," as opposed to a text strictly for lawyers. Despite it being about fashion law, the end-game was to create a book that a person either already engaged in, or seeking to engage in, a fashion business could comprehend and immediately utilize by providing the reader with a straightforward understanding of the law with limited *legalese*. The result would ideally be that they could now actually apply the law to their own business, whether if trying to make sense of a basic garment labeling issue, or attempting to determine a more complex matter, such as how to lawfully import exotic animal skins for an accessories line.

Given the number of people looking to get into the fashion industry, whether diving in full-time as a young entrepreneur, a mid-career person taking on a "side hustle," or a baby boomer setting up their next "job," it seemed unfair to me that in order to get the basic answers, you either had to hire a lawyer, or hope to find the answer you were looking for on an Etsy® discussion thread due to there not being one central location where a gamut of answers to the most commonly sought questions could be found. This collection of foundational legal know-how and practical application is what this book aims to accomplish.

A global business approach

The second goal I aimed to achieve with the book's design was that it had to incorporate the laws that account for the ever pervasive global dimension of the fashion industry. As an attorney for fifteen years, with a majority of those working with domestic sellers and importers of fashion merchandise, as well as a professor of International Business Law and International Business Transactions at New York City's Fashion Institute of Technology (SUNY FIT), and Business

Law at LIM College in its former MBA program (i.e., collectively teaching for nearly ten years), I found there was a severe deficit in materials for teaching the laws governing fashion merchandise and the companies selling it. This was especially so in relation to incorporating the global aspect of the fashion industry when you consider that roughly one-third of all imports into the US was (and still is) categorized as either wearing apparel or a textile product.

Due to a series of consumer product safety law amendments that became enforceable in 2009–2010, US importers now more than ever need to understand the importance of record-keeping measures, testing protocols, and instructing their foreign suppliers on the organization and completion of certain documents to ensure their own (the importer's) compliance with the law. Couple this with the rise in internet advertising and sales capabilities, the ease in creating a storefront website through a template and integrated payment systems, and shifts in e-commerce shipping to make global business all the more accessible, the doors were opened for entrepreneurs to join in the industry with just a few clicks. In my mind, this convergence of factors made it all the more critical to have a practical text on the market to support the growing numbers of entrepreneurs in the US as well as those overseas who were seeking to prepare their merchandise to be US market ready.

Coverage

This book is organized to account for the product-specific laws sellers of fashion merchandise must abide by, the marketing, importing and exporting laws governing such products, and the top legal compliance and governance issues a fashion business must consider. It also includes considerations for working with transportation providers, utilizing intellectual property to protect a brand and its profits, and approaches to incorporating sustainable practices into any business. Comprehensively, this text accomplishes what I aimed to create five years ago, and I hope you will find it provides you with a legal roadmap for business success. Additional resources to accompany this text may be accessed at www.fashioncompliance.com.

Chapter 1

Fashion law for a global industry

When you examine an industry from a comprehensive point of view, the interconnected nature of people and processes acting in concert together is unveiled. In the context of fashion, we find industry participants extend well beyond that of designers, big brands, and retailers. Be it the advertising executives whose work product lures us to the retailers, the sales people at the stores we love to shop at, the workers who make the components used in clothing, the manufacturers, importers, truckers, vessel/rail/air carriers, and even the cotton farmers that make wearing natural fibers possible, it brings to light the industry's massive impact as the number of people employed in the industry worldwide is enormous. In addition, each of these individuals are consumers themselves.

Learning objectives

- Understand the legal framework unique to a fashion business
- Identify the most significant government agencies regulating fashion
- Describe the importance of a fashion compliance program
- Recognize when it is time to engage legal counsel

Fashion's legal framework

This text will analyze the legal framework governing this global industry, as well as the parties to whom the law applies. Through an examination of the breadth of participants and laws, one can begin to understand the complexity of both the fashion business and the laws governing its operations as multiple legal obligations imposed by different government **administrative agencies** (which are governmental bodies with the authority to implement and administer particular legislation) converge on a day-to-day basis. Such primary agencies include:

- US Federal Trade Commission
- US Consumer Product Safety Commission
- US Fish and Wildlife
- US Customs and Border Protection
- US Department of Commerce
- US Patent and Trademark Office
- US Copyright Office of the Library of Congress.

As you will read, this book is organized into chapters which describe in detail the application and purpose of the legal mandate administered by these agencies in their regulation and enforcement of the federal laws for which their agency has a specific oversight.

The timeframes to consider for legal compliance

Fashion merchandise produced in the US must be compliant with US law at the time it is ready to be offered for sale. Since US laws are applicable within the US only, as a general proposition, products made in other countries destined for sale in the US do not need to be compliant with US laws until the time of importation into the US. This means that a product could be manufactured, packaged, and transported in a foreign location without being 100 percent compliant with US law as it is not within the US. Despite being made abroad however, a US importer is still responsible for instructing its foreign manufacturer to undertake such necessary activities to render the goods it intends to import compliant with US law. For this reason, while the legal requirement may not exist until a certain future date, i.e., until the time of importation, activities leading to the result of compliance such as product testing, may actually need to occur several months in advance of such future deadline.

The US system of federal and state law

State laws can impact how fashion merchandise is sold, such as where the attachment of a California "Proposition 65 warning label" is required,[1] or even impact a firm's business operations, such as the New York State requirement for apparel manufacturers to annually register with the New York State Department of Labor so it may monitor labor relations and prevent garment sweatshops.[2] Given the nuances amongst state laws however, this book focuses on the federal laws put forth by the US Congress, and the regulations created and enforced by the various US federal government agencies. Specific state laws should always, of course, be identified and abided by when operating within that state.

The US has a dual system of both federal law and state law, with the former being created by the federal government, and the latter by a state's government. While federal laws are applicable across and within each of the fifty states and the US territories, each state likewise has a legal system governing what are considered state law issues, such as that of obtaining a driver's license. While it may sound complex to have two sets of laws, a simple example can help to demystify it.

One highly visible pair of federal and state laws is that governing wages. The federal minimum wage is, and has been since 2009, $7.25 per hour as of the publishing of this book.[3] Generally speaking, it is lower than that of a state's minimum wage, as is the case with the State of New York whose minimum hourly wage is either $10.50 or $11.00 per hour, depending on the number of employees a business has.[4]

The purpose of statutes and regulations

The US Congress, which is made up of the US House of Representatives and the US Senate, writes the federal laws which are known individually as a **statute.** These laws are thereafter converted into **regulations** which allow a federal government agency, including those mentioned above, to implement the laws drafted by Congress. Generally speaking, the regulations

1 define the scope of what a particular law covers,

2 identifies who is subject to complying with the law,

3 states how compliance with the law can be achieved,

4 lists what records need to be kept to demonstrate that compliance has occurred, and

5 indicates the punitive measures, whether monetary penalties, imprisonment, or other enforcement activities, which result from a failure to comply with the law.

Every existing business has a responsibility to follow the law. With respect to the fashion industry, this can be achieved through a company-centric compliance program to ensure adherence to the laws applicable to its business.

One's obligation to know the law

In 2016, more than $121.5 billion worth of wearing apparel and textile products were imported into the United States from around the world.[5] Recognizing the interconnectedness of foreign labor and materials to domestically sold merchandise, **fashion law**, as used in this book, is the compilation of several bodies of law that collectively regulate such sales of fashion merchandise and those entities engaged in facilitating this commercial activity. This broad definition is used for the simple fact that fashion law must be viewed, understood, and studied within the realm of actual business operations.

Global and domestic sellers of fashion merchandise have an obligation to know what legal requirements their products must comply with in order to be imported, sold, distributed, and even given away for free, lawfully. Issues can arise in relation to the laws governing mandatory labeling and fiber disclosures, product testing, and the crafting of non-deceptive marketing claims, such as a garment being "Eco-friendly."

Due to the financial risks that can arise from non-compliance with the law which can result in penalties equaling tens of thousands of dollars, making sense of which agency is regulating what activity and how to operate lawfully is critical for a business's survival. Non-compliance risks aside, there are several other business operations which by their very nature can give rise to legal implications, such as

- negotiating a retail lease,
- hiring employees whether full-time or part-time; or
- engaging independent contractors, including
  - models,
  - companies who set up the runways for a fashion show,
  - consultants and others providing vendor oversight, e.g., over factories,
  - transportation providers, and
  - warehouses.

As each of these involve legalities that could give rise to financial or other consequences, for purposes of learning about fashion law this book will challenge you to think about a fashion business from a multi-dimensional and interconnected point of view, as actions done in one area of a business can readily trigger legal obligations in another part of it. The laws analyzed in this book relate to

- consumer product safety,
- product labeling,
- business formation,
- marketing,
- intellectual property,
- international trade,
- transportation and shipping, and
- labor.

As other texts cover in great detail areas concerning the laws relating to the people and processes for actually making a sale, whether in terms of retail leases or employment issues, such as that of the Kolsun and Jimenez text by Bloomsbury Publishing entitled *Fashion Law*,[6] this book takes a product-centric and global operations legal compliance focus in its analysis and coverage of the laws governing a fashion enterprise.

Lastly, no business could operate on a long-term basis oblivious to the social and environmental concerns that permeate industry norms—at least not anymore. Given the pervasive use of subcontracted overseas labor in the fashion industry, legal considerations for creating an "ethical code of labor conduct" and forming a corporate entity as one mandated to provide a social and environmental benefit, are additional areas included under the umbrella of fashion law and compliance which are covered in this book.

Fashion compliance: Translating legal obligations into business practices

Fashion compliance means abiding by the laws that regulate a business in the fashion industry. These laws will vary for each entity based on the activity they are engaged in within the industry. For example, an online retailer of men's underwear will be subject to complying with fewer regulations then a physical children's wear store. In approaching how to implement a fashion compliance program, it can be thought of in two components:

1 knowing what the applicable regulations are as determined by the type of merchandise sold, how it is sold, and to whom the intended consumer is; and

2 implementing protocols to comply with the state and federal laws governing these products.

Elements of a fashion compliance program

A basic fashion compliance program is one where there are internal controls and procedures for implementing the measures of such laws and regulations an entity must adhere to in its day-to-day operations. This information should be in written form and regularly updated so that new and existing employees can understand the tasks that must be done. It should also be periodically amended to reflect adjustments to practices which enable a company's ongoing compliance with any revised laws.

The importance of written procedures

Where a government agency decides to investigate or audit a business to ensure compliance with its regulations, the first thing it wants to know about is the company's compliance program to the extent one exists. For the agency to assess whether a company has been aware of its regulations and understands its compliance obligations, procedures need to be in writing and a compliance manual is one of the first documents requested in an audit. In addition to this, the agency will evaluate if a company's own procedures (as written) had been followed, including where errors had been identified and corrected, or if instead such issues were known, or should have been known, but a company did nothing to remedy them. This failure to exercise due diligence could result in what a government agency may view as a violation of their rules, and ultimately lead to penalties or other punitive measures.

The fashion compliance manual

A simple and effective way to maintain information on a company's fashion compliance program is by creating a manual. To get started in designing one, it should set forth a company's basic standard operations and, where also an importer or exporter, should also include the details around any import and export procedures. Information contained in a fashion compliance manual should specifically:

- Include a basic description about the business and its product lines.

- Identify the vendors from whom products are purchased and details on its service providers.

- Describe any standard protocols for ordering, invoicing, and shipping.

- Contain separate sections relating to each administrative agency with details about how its regulations apply to a company's products and business operations, and within each of these sections provide a description of measures implemented for legal compliance purposes.

- Explain how the company ensures its ongoing compliance with the law, e.g., by conducting a periodic internal review of its business practices.

The manual should be specific to your company

A compliance program must be designed around a company's actual operations. To be an effective compliance program internal controls and procedures need to be actively implemented and revised, with key personnel updated on changes in practices. Having an effective program is strengthened when there is a culture of accountability in which individuals understand the concept of compliance and their role within the compliance chain. Remember, surviving in today's market requires protecting against risks. By having a fashion compliance program a business can ensure it knows the laws applicable to the merchandise it is selling and the business it is operating. As a prudent measure, it is recommended to periodically consult with an attorney to ensure the manual is updated with the current law, and that existing company operations remain sufficient to meet compliance obligations.

When to use a lawyer

While avoiding legal troubles should always be a priority, inevitably a growing business will need to retain an attorney at some point. From handling immediate crises, to managing long term business disruptions, to simply getting a company on the right track, attorneys can help clients make sense of which laws their company needs to abide by, identify problem areas so they can be fixed, and redirect internal practices so that risks and liabilities are minimized. Lawyers in the fashion industry may be hired to resolve a specific problem, identify and eliminate threats, review and write contracts, protect assets, evaluate business opportunities, and generally help people and companies grow their business in a way that enables them to run their operations more efficiently and with greater confidence.

Hire a lawyer who can see the "big picture"

Any major decision a company makes will typically impact another area of the business, be it a reallocation of internal resources or a change in a company's finances. When evaluating counsel, it is important to recognize that while attorneys are generally knowledgeable about a specific area of law, they should nonetheless be able to articulate to a business how their services, and the associated costs, fit into a company's overall plans. With so many laws to be aware of, your typical fashion business needs an expert who understands more than the specific rules and regulations you initially go to them about. That is not to say they should be an expert in several areas of law, as given the complexities of the law that is not realistic. An ability to take a high-level look at a business however, to identify implications and potential ramifications on it that may result from work performed by the attorney, should be a skill that they possess. They should also have an ability to provide some flexibility in terms of the way the work is managed in order to meet the cash flow realities most fashion businesses face. This could mean breaking up a project into phases, doing one contract at a time, offering a payment plan, or some other solution.

How law firm's charge for their services

There is no faster way of being disappointed with an attorney than by being surprised by their fees and the resulting bill. Be advised however, that lawyers are expensive. When searching for legal services, an understanding of the company's own budget in relation to how much an attorney costs should be considered. As an aside, I have heard several stories about startups raising funding only to unwittingly use a law firm whose fees amount to more than half of the funding the startup had raised. As a resource who comes to know the intimate details regarding your business, your relationship with your attorney should be one built on trust and transparency, and not on the self-serving interests on the part of either the company or the lawyer. Questions must therefore be asked about fees, including whether the attorney charges by the hour, has a flat fee structure, or a combination of both. Depending on the service, for example, a business formation or the preparation and filing of a trademark application, a flat fee may be charged. For handling a lawsuit however, fees will more likely be calculated under an hourly billable arrangement, as would be the analysis or drafting of a contract. For legal billing purposes, the hour is broken into ten (10) six minute (6 min.) increments. Six minutes of legal services is quantified into the legal charge of 0.1. The legal fee associated with this is therefore:

0.1 × attorney cost per hour (aka, the *hourly billing rate*)

If your lawyer costs $300 per hour, for 0.1 or six minutes of their time, the cost would be $30. This is a reality of the profession both in the US and several countries abroad, and phone calls are typically recorded at a minimum of 0.1, even if the call is for less time. Not all attorneys charge for phone calls however, so be sure to inquire about what time is, and is not, charged by your attorney, as well as which expenses, such as photocopies, are ultimately added to an invoice. Lastly, bear in mind that a significant investment in time and money has been made by an attorney in order to serve in this capacity. Trying to negotiate lower rates in advance of retaining counsel, especially when attempting to retain a seasoned attorney, or attempting to obtain free legal advice through a litany of questions during a phone call, are generally attitudes recognized as disrespectful, and this behavior should be avoided.

That being said, given the costs, a reiteration on the point about retaining an attorney who has an ability to see the bigger picture is warranted. A business needs counsel who can see the legal issues and the overall impact their own work will have on a company because often times a business owner and corporate officers cannot ascertain such impacts on their own, or may not know which questions to ask in order to form any reasonable conclusion. A good lawyer will not merely be one-dimensional and self-serving, but will be in a position to direct you to other counsel who may assist with other legal issues a business may or may not be aware of that are in need of resolution. In addition, attorneys can also be used to help with capturing new opportunities, such as with licensing, as explained in the next section.

Using the law to capture opportunities

Licensing is the sale of a license authorizing another to use something, such as one's intellectual property (IP).[7] **Intellectual property** generally refers to creations of the mind, that is, creative works or ideas embodied in a shareable form which can enable others to re-create, emulate or manufacture them.[8] In terms of fashion, such IP is most commonly a trademark or copyright, and in the fashion industry it often takes the form of a logo, design, character, or other graphic, as discussed in greater detail in Chapter 3.

From Vera Wang® dishes to Missoni® home interiors, we have seen companies extend their brands beyond their core products to capitalize on new sales channels which enjoy success due, in part, to the brand's already existing recognition. While some companies may consider adding on an expanded product line and independently exploring new sales channels themselves, these new avenues are typically exploited through licensing.

Licensing can begin after an agreement has been made between the entity which owns the IP, known as the **licensor**, and the party leasing its use, which is the **licensee**. The contract would cover details such as how the IP would be used, including on which types of products it would be placed, where in the world such products may be distributed, and at what price range such goods incorporating the IP may be sold. A license agreement is only good for the time period stated in the contract and importantly, may be used only by such parties designated within it.

When is the right time to license your intellectual property?

A licensor typically receives both a flat fee from the licensee for the right to use the IP, for example, a brand's name, in addition to a portion of the proceeds of each sale of the product upon which the IP is placed, or otherwise used. A licensor therefore has every incentive to begin the licensing process as soon as it is advantageous to do so. As stated in the strategies for brand management and licensing by Bill D'Arienzo in Box 1.1, there is an optimal time to begin licensing for which the strategy for doing so should be looked at from an external, internal, and operational brand management approach.

Box 1.1 Brand management and licensing strategies by Bill D'Arienzo of WDA Marketing

Licensing is the renting of IP assets to another company which has the core competencies to manufacture and distribute a product category which the brand owner neither wants to produce or has the capacity to successfully market; the decision to do so should be approached strategically. This is made up of three interdependent brand management components: external, internal, and operational.

Strategic licensing: External brand management

- Licensing should be undertaken when the brand and its signature product is on the ascendency, preferably when all three measures of growth (market share, revenue, and profits) indicate you are a market leader. Too often, this is not the case, as licensing appears as an easy revenue generator.

- Licensing should never be seen as a generator of revenue alone; it should be understood as part of other business objectives such as:

  o increasing brand awareness;

  o partnering with licensees that have strong unique strengths (e.g. retail channel relationships) that the brand owner does not have;

  o market entry into foreign or new geographies, product categories or consumer segments.

- Strategic licensing also may include prohibiting access to a market or channel of a significant competing brand.

- In all instances above, brand extensions in the form of licensing have to be organic extensions of the product/brand category for which the brand owner is a market leader. Here the concept of lifestyle comes into play.

  o The clearer the consumer perception that the mother brand has positioned itself as a lifestyle brand, the more likely it is that the new licensee (all other things being equal) will find acceptance as an authentic extension of the brand's promise and values.

  o The determination of what constitutes a lifestyle brand cannot be simply the assertion of such by the brand manager but needs to be confirmed by the market through the fashion media, online communities, and internet influencers. This needs to be framed over time through ads and images which portrayed brand and product in settings and situations which define a certain style of life (think Ralph Lauren New England Brahmins or Michael Kors Jet Set). Still, there are caveats.

    So for a brand owner to enter menswear without any alignment with their women's sportswear brand is a risky strategy as leveraging the mother brand's equity as a strategic advantage is reduced when consumers are unfamiliar with the association between the brand and the product category; trusting and therefore testing the product is compromised (witness Harley Davidson licensing its brand for neckties or toothpaste!).

In this regard, studies have shown that luxury brands are able to stretch the organic connection more than mass brands, as the equity they possess is deeper in the consumers perception of trust and authenticity.

Strategic licensing: Internal brand management

External brand management, to be successful, needs to be anchored in the culture of the company that owns the brand. This needs to be in place prior to marketing the brand for licensing. Each of the functionalities (i.e., Sourcing, Manufacturing, Design, Merchandising, Sales, Marketing and Finance) must understand the brand's values and its archetype as the foundation and the unifying principal in guiding internal business decisions. They all should speak in one brand language, embrace the brand's written mission statement, and strive to realize the brand's written vision statement as well. Successful internal brand marketing is the pre-condition for successful external brand marketing.

These brand attributes become the basis for identifying and assessing the proper fit with potential licensees. Licensees must see the business through the kaleidoscope of the brand and be able to consistently execute its mission and identity in product, packaging, placement/distribution, and pricing; for online, the same adherence must occur in conversations, content, context, and online communities.

The brand owners marketing team will need to develop media kits and brand books both of which will provide the licensee with guardrails as to the appropriate use of IP assets and images for marketing communications helping to ensure a brand consistency across all product categories.

Strategic licensing: Operational brand management

The final capability which must be in place prior to undertaking a licensing strategy is to have an internal operational licensing team and monitoring procedures. Licensing partners will have to adhere to brand guidelines in product development, distribution channels, and image marketing and meet certain minimums in terms of sales goals and royalty rates. These latter financial obligations are contractual and licensees must meet quarterly and annual minimums and affect timely payments of royalties to the brand owner. Their shipments will need to be audited by the brand managers by reviewing invoices to ensure that appropriate pricing and distribution standards, as stated in the contract, have been met.

Licensees must also adhere to time and action calendars to meet seasonal product releases and be guided by the latest market trends that brand owners are embracing. Story boards with color and themes presented for review must be part of the on-going process of monitoring each licensees pre-production brand strategy. Brand marketing in support of the seasonal collections will also, at this juncture, be presented and subject to review and sign-off by brand management.

To sum up, the legal framework governing the fashion enterprise is a complex blend of state and federal law. It further is unique to every company, as the applicability of the law turns on factors such as the type of business the entity is engaged in, the type of products sold, how the merchandise is sold, where it originates from, and for whom a product is ultimately to be used by.

The analysis presented over the remainder of this book will enable an identification of the primary legal areas a company in the business of fashion should be paying attention to. It will also help you to think about which factors, including those mentioned directly above, are in need of analysis in relation to the above-enumerated administrative agencies, each of which is discussed in detail throughout the remaining chapters of this book. By the end of this book you should have a solid understanding of the laws that must be assessed against a business operating in the fashion industry, and be ready to prepare your own fashion compliance manual across the different legal areas, whether as would be applicable to your own business, or that for which you are employed.

Key terms	fashion law	licensor
	intellectual property	regulation
administrative agencies	licensee	statute
duty	licensing	
fashion compliance		

Discussion questions and exercises

1 Choose one of your favorite fashion brands and after researching the company, identify two products you think would be complementary to their core product offering for purposes of licensing and explain the basis for your answer. For example, the Burberry® brand has as its core product the raincoat. A recommendation for licensing would be to license the brand to companies

that sell umbrellas and gloves, which both are products that complement a raincoat offering.[9]

2 Describe the elements of a fashion compliance program and explain the importance of having one.

3 Imagine you are tasked with hiring an attorney for your company to help with drafting a contract. Prepare a list of questions you would ask the attorney to ensure they would be a good fit for your business.

Notes

1. *See,* Cal Heath & Safety Code 25249.8. California's Safe Drinking Water and Toxic Enforcement Act, commonly known as "Proposition 65," requires a business to warn people about significant amounts of chemicals in the products they make where that chemical is both known to cause cancer, birth defects or other reproductive harm and is listed on the "Prop 65 list." In its simplest terms, it requires a product label where the levels considered safe are exceeded.
2. https://labor.ny.gov/workerprotection/laborstandards/workprot/sweatshp.shtm (last viewed July 12, 2017).
3. https://www.dol.gov/whd/minimumwage.htm (last viewed July 13, 2017).
4. https://labor.ny.gov/workerprotection/laborstandards/workprot/lshmpg.shtm (last viewed July 12, 2017).
5. *Textiles and Wearing Apparel Brochure, US Customs Office of Trade, Textiles and Wearing Apparel,* CBP Publication #0586–1116, https://www.cbp.gov/sites/default/files/assets/documents/2016-Dec/FY%202016%20-%20Textiles_PTI%20Brochure.pdf (last viewed May 28, 2017).
6. *Fashion Law: A Guide for Designers, Fashion Executives, & Attorneys,* 2nd edition, Fairchild Books, an imprint of Bloomsbury Publishing, 2014.
7. *See, Black's Law Dictionary,* 7th edition, West Group, p. 932, 1999.
8. https://www.uspto.gov/learning-and-resources/general-faqs#1242 (viewed on October 30, 2016).
9. Bill D'Arienzo shared this example with the author in 2013.

Chapter 2

Consumer safety and product labeling guidance

Details about a product's composition are found on virtually all consumer goods whether printed directly onto a product, or embodied in a sticker, hang tag, or a sewn-in label attached to it. The labeling laws which mandate such disclosures are intended to protect and inform consumers and in the case of wearing apparel, there are three primary laws which govern such labeling. Namely, the Textile Fiber Products Identification Act (15 USC §70 et seq.) ("TFPIA"), the Wool Products Labeling Act (15 USC §68 et seq.) ("WPLA"), and the Fur Products Labeling Act (15 USC §69 et seq.) ("FPLA"), of which the first two will be the focus of this chapter given the enormity of the use of these fibers in fashion merchandise.

Learning objectives

- Understand which disclosures are required on wearing apparel and accessories
- Identify what the exceptions are to the labeling requirements
- Recognize when an "RN#" may be used on a label
- Know where and how labels must be attached to merchandise

Labeling legalities

The laws governing mandatory label disclosures have three broad and collective goals:

1 To prevent unnecessary harm which could result from using a product.

2 To enable consumers to care for their purchases.

3 To prevent deceptive or false representations about a product, including that of what materials a garment is made out of.

In this respect, while the TFPIA, WPLA and FPLA each have their own requirements, many parallel rules are shared across the three laws in terms of the labeling of fiber disclosures. The Federal Trade Commission (FTC) has oversight of the federal labeling requirements for textile, wool, and fur products and is the agency responsible for enforcing compliance with these laws.[1]

Merchandise subject to the TFPIA and WPLA labeling laws are largely wearing apparel, accessories worn on the body, and consumer goods found in the home. Products governed by the TFPIA are known as **textile fiber products**, which are any fiber or yarn, in either a finished or unfinished state, that is used or intended for use in a **household textile article** ("HTA"), and is not a product containing wool as those are governed by the WPLA. An HTA is a textile good of a type customarily used in a household regardless of where in fact it is used. Examples of an HTA include draperies, floor coverings, furnishings, beddings, costumes and accessories, and of course, wearing apparel.

Products governed by the WPLA are known as **wool products**[2] which are any product, or portion of a product, which contains or in any way is represented as containing **wool**, which is the fiber from the fleece of the sheep or lamb, the hair of the Angora or Cashmere goat, or the specialty fibers from the hair of the camel, alpaca, llama, or vicuna.[3] Wool can also encompass an item containing **recycled wool**, which is either (1) the resulting fiber when wool has been woven or felted into a wool product which, without ever having been utilized in any way by the ultimate consumer, subsequently has been made into a fibrous state, or (2) the resulting fiber when wool or reprocessed wool has been spun, woven, knitted, or felted into a wool product which, after having been used in any way by an ultimate consumer, is subsequently made into a fibrous state.[4]

The general requirements for label disclosures

The general requirement for fiber disclosures on both textile and wool products is that each article has a **label**, whether a stamp, tag, label, or other means of identification affixed to it.[5] The label must be affixed securely and contain all of the regulatory mandated information ("Required Information") in a legible, conspicuous, and non-deceptive format. Where instructions must be provided to the factory actually labeling the products, it is important to note that in the event of an error, the FTC views the instructing party as responsible for any improperly labeled goods, and therefore any allegation of wrongdoing would be made against such company, e.g., the brand who instructed its manufacturer, and not the factory itself.

English language requirement

All Required Information must be in English and where goods are imported, the English name of the country where processed or manufactured must be provided.[6] Variant spelling that clearly indicates the English name of the country, such as "Brasil" for Brazil is acceptable, as are unmistakably clear abbreviations such as "Gt. Britain" for "Great Britain." The adjectival form of the name of the country, e.g., "China" to "Chinese," may also be used.[7]

Placement and permanency requirement of label information

Every label containing Required Information must be conspicuous, securely affixed to a product, its package or container, and also of such durability as to remain attached throughout any distribution until sold and delivered to the ultimate consumer.[8]

Labeling of pairs or products containing two or more units

The way in which Required Information is placed on the packaging of a product containing two or more units, e.g., socks, turns on whether or not it can be clearly seen through the packaging itself. With textile fiber products, provided they are marketed and delivered in a package which is intended to remain unbroken and intact until after delivery to the ultimate consumer, are in transparent packaging, and the label containing Required Information is clearly visible, no package label is required, and conversely, where packaging cannot be seen through, it is.[9]

With respect to wool products, where a package consists of two or more parts, units, or items of different fiber content, a separate label containing the Required Information must be affixed to each of them.[10] Where multiple products are marketed or sold collectively as a single product, it may instead be set out on a single label that distinguishes the fiber composition of each part, unit, or item.[11]

Products subject to following the textile and wool label rules[12]

Most clothing and textile products commonly used in a household are subject to either the TFPIA or WPLA rules. **Wearing apparel** is defined under the TFPIA as any costume, article of clothing, or covering for any part of the body worn or intended to be worn by individuals. While the WPLA does not define wearing apparel, such is almost identically defined under the Flammable Fabrics Act (see Chapter 5) for which wool products worn on an individual are covered.

Making fiber content disclosures

There are specific regulations governing which fiber names may be used in a disclosure, when they are used, and how their presence must be indicated on a label. The FTC has a specific list of fiber terms for use on labels and in 2014 expanded their approved fiber list to incorporate fibers listed in "ISO–2076: 2010(E)" which is a publication by the International Standards Organization ("ISO") entitled, "Textiles—Man Made Fibres—Generic Names," and has since been revised by the ISO to "ISO–2076: 2013" under the same title. A copy of this publication may be purchased at the ISO website at www.iso.org.[13]

Using generic fiber names

When provided as Required Information, the generic names of all fibers present in either, (a) an amount of 5 percent or more of the total fiber weight of a textile fiber product or, (b) all wool fibers present in *any* amount, must be stated, for example as "cotton," "rayon," "silk," "linen," "nylon," "wool," "recycled wool," etc.[14] For manufactured fibers, the FTC has approved the generic fiber names in Box 2.1, for whose definitions may be found on the FTC website at www.ftc.gov.

Rule to use generic names with fiber trademarks[16]

Some companies prefer to use a trademarked fiber name (TFN) on their products when stating Required Information, such as Lycra®, Tencel® or Cupro®. This is permissible as long as the TFN is stated together with the generic name of the fiber to which it relates, appears close to the generic name in type or lettering of equal size and conspicuousness, and contains a full and complete fiber content disclosure.

Box 2.1 Current FTC approved generic terms[15] (not including ISO 2076:2013 fibers)

Acetate	Lastol	Polyethylene
Acrylic	Lastrile	Polyimide
Alginate	Lyocell	Polypropylene
Anidex	Metal Fibre	Rayon
Aramid	Metallic	Rubber
Azlon	Modacrylic	Saran
Carbon	Modal	Spandex
Chlorofibre	Novoloid	Sulfar
Cupro	Nylon	Triacetate
Elastane	Nytril	Vinal
Elasterell-p	Olefin	Vinylal
Elastodiene	PBI	Vinyon
Elastoester	PLA	Viscose
Fluorofibre	Polyamide	
Glass	Polyester	

Where a fiber trademark is placed on a label for reasons other than disclosing Required Information, such as for marketing purposes, the generic name(s) of the fibers do not need to accompany the TFN.[17] The only caveat is that where a product contains multiple fibers and has a hang tag denoting only the TFN or what would otherwise be an incomplete list of fibers, then the hang tag must disclose clearly and conspicuously that it does not provide the product's full fiber content e.g., "See label for the product's full fiber content."[18]

Listing fibers in order of predominance[19]

For textile fiber products, any disclosure of a single fiber that is 5 percent or more of a garment's total fiber content in proportion to the whole must be listed

1 by its TFN and/or generic name(s);
2 in the order of the predominant fiber by weight;

3 state the percentages by weight of each fiber present (excluding permissive ornamentation), and

4 designate fiber(s) less than 5 percent of the total fiber weight as "other fiber" or "other fibers" and appear last in the sequence of fiber disclosures.

A sample label illustrating how fibers should be listed in order of predominance is provided in Figure 2.1.

Sectional disclosures of fiber content[20]

Where a textile fiber or wool product is composed of two or more sections that are of different fiber composition, such disclosure may be separated in the same label to show the fiber composition of each section, as shown in Figure 2.2.

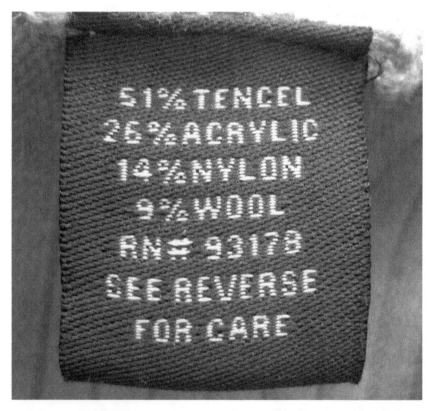

Figure 2.1 Label with fibers listed in the order of predominance. Source: Deanna Clark-Esposito.

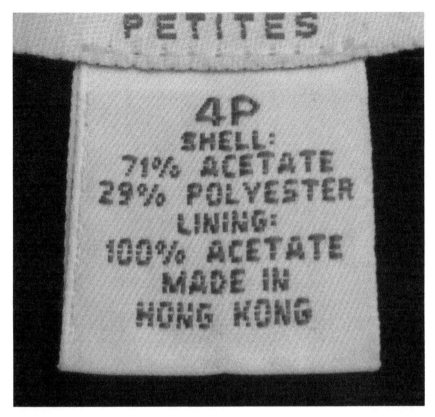

Figure 2.2 Label stating the sectional fiber content disclosures. Source: Deanna Clark-Esposito.

Tolerated variances in fiber content claims[21]

Where a textile fiber product contains multiple fibers, the disclosed fiber content in its stated percentage may deviate by no more than 3 percent from its actual amount. For example, where the label indicates that a particular fiber is present in the amount of 40 percent, such fiber may in fact vary from a minimum of 37 percent to a maximum of 43 percent of the total fiber weight. This rule applies to all fibers except those considered "ornamentation," as described more fully later in this chapter, since its disclosure is not required under the rules when less than 5 percent and there is more than one fiber in the product. When made up solely of one fiber however, this deviation exception does not apply and should be represented as being composed of one fiber "exclusive of ornamentation." It should be noted that the WPLA has no such parallel regulation for wool products.

Pile fabric disclosures

The fiber content of pile fabrics, like velvet, or products composed of them, should be stated individually on the label, indicating the face or pile fibers and those of the back or base, with their percentages.[22] For example, "100% Nylon Pile, 100% Cotton Back (Back constitutes 60% of fabric and pile 40%)."

Fiber disclosures when product composed of miscellaneous cloth scraps[23]

With eco-fashion designers experimenting with ways to take what would ordinarily be factory waste and creating wearing apparel and accessories from it, it follows that labels regarding scraps and unknown fibers may rise in usage than they have been historically. For wool products made from miscellaneous cloth scraps containing various fibers of undetermined percentages, the label can indicate a minimum percentage of wool e.g., "Made of Miscellaneous Cloth Scraps Composed Chiefly of Cotton With Minimum of __% Recycled Wool." It may be confusing as to why a fiber may be unknown, however, where a label has been removed about the fiber content, or in the case of scraps being sold in a secondary market, such information may simply never have been retained, and therefore the buyer (in our example of the eco-fashion designer) would have no reason to know what the true fibers and their percentages had actually been.

Labeling textile fiber products containing unknown fabrics

Whether the types of fibers are completely unknown or partially unknown, the TFPIA regulations offer select labeling options to convey when a product is made from rags, miscellaneous scraps, odd lots, secondhand materials, textile by-products, or waste materials of unknown, and for practical purposes, undeterminable fiber content.[24] In the case where fibers are 100 percent unknown, rather than listing all of the assumed fibers, the disclosure may state for example, "All undetermined fibers—textile by-products," "Secondhand materials—fiber content unknown," or "Made of miscellaneous scraps of undetermined fiber content." Where a portion of the fibers are both known and unknown, the disclosure of the undeterminable fiber content together with a percentage disclosure of any known or determinable fibers should be made in accordance with the general requirement to disclose the fiber content.[25] An example of such a label is, "50% Rayon, 50% Secondhand Materials—Fiber Content Unknown."

Labeling wearing apparel made of remnants[26]

Remnants are portions of fabric severed from their bolts or rolls where the fiber content of such piece of fabric may be known or unknown. When wearing apparel is, for all practical purposes, made of remnants for which the fiber content is unknown or undeterminable, fibers may be disclosed as, "Made of remnants of undetermined fiber content." It should be noted that where any disclosure of a portion of the fiber content that is known is made, then it is no longer permissible to use such language and known fibers must be disclosed.

Marking sample products, swatches and specimens

Fiber content disclosures and other Required Information are mandated on both textile and wool product samples, swatches, or specimens where used to promote or effect sales. In the case of textile products, exceptions to this labeling rule exist where the sample is less than two square inches in area and the information is conspicuously disclosed on accompanying promotional materials, are keyed to a catalog to which reference may be readily made, and is necessary to complete the sale of the products.[27] When, however, a textile product is not in a form intended for sale, delivery to, or for use by the ultimate consumer, rather than individually labeling it, the fiber content identifying the proportional percentages to the whole may be detailed on an invoice or other document, provided it shows the name and address of the person issuing such document and all other Required Information.[28] Unfortunately, under the WPLA, wool products are not permitted to use this form of alternate labeling, and therefore must always contain an individual label.

Exceptions to the fiber disclosure requirement

The textile and wool rules differ slightly when it comes to the three primary exceptions to the general requirement to disclose fiber content. They are ornamentation, trimmings, and products containing linings, interlinings, fillings and paddings. In addition, a fourth exception, as explained further below, also exists with certain household textile articles that are simply exempt by virtue of being a particular product.

Ornamentation exception[29]

Under the TFPIA, the fiber content of **ornamentation**, which is defined as any fibers or yarns imparting a visibly discernible pattern or design to a yarn or fabric, must be disclosed only when it is more than 5 percent of the total fiber weight of a product. For wool ornamentation however, even where less than 5 percent, wool fibers must be disclosed. When containing ornamentation, labels may state "exclusive of ornamentation" or, in the case of wool, use a more specific statement detailing the fibers where the basic disclosure is made, for example, "All Alpaca, Exclusive of Ornamentation."[30] As an option, ornamentation may also be disclosed where its percentage in relation to the total fiber weight of the principal fiber(s) is known, for example, "100% Wool, Exclusive of 3% Silk Ornamentation."

Trimming exception

Trimmings made of textile fibers that do not exceed 15 percent of the surface area of the wearing apparel or other household textile article are exempt from the requirement to disclose its fiber content. However, where made of wool, no such product exemption exists and therefore must be disclosed.[31] Trimming types include, but are not limited to, tape, gussets, cuffs, braids, labels, findings, and decorative trim.[32]

Products containing linings, interlinings, fillings and paddings

The fiber content disclosure of any linings, interlinings, fillings, or paddings is not normally required for a textile fiber product unless (1) an express or implied representation is made as to their fiber content, or (2) it has been incorporated into the product for warmth rather than for structural purposes.[33] Where the latter, they must be labeled separately and distinctly, e.g., "100% Nylon, Interlining: 100% Rayon, Covering: 100% Rayon, Filling: 100% Cotton." Where **interlinings**, i.e., any fabric or fibers incorporated into an article of wearing apparel as a layer between an outer shell and an inner lining, are present, the fiber content of such interlinings must also be set forth separately and distinctly.[34]

Products not subject to TFPIA disclosure unless fiber data volunteered[35]

In addition to the three exceptions explained above, certain HTAs also do not require disclosing a product's fiber unless textile fiber information is voluntarily provided on the product itself or in an advertisment. Such items include, but are not limited to, belts, shoe laces, garters, and secondhand clothing which are discernibly secondhand, or which are marked to indicate their secondhand character.[36]

The only instance where this fourth exception would not apply is where a fiber has a clearly established and definite functional significance. For example, where an article contains spandex, the label would need to state its quantity, e.g., "96 percent Acetate, 4 percent Spandex."[37] It should be noted that this rule only applies to textile fiber products that do not contain wool or recycled wool as irrespective of its percentage, wool fibers must always be disclosed by their generic name or TFN.

Use of term "All" or "100%"[38]

The term "All" or "100%" may be used under certain conditions, and interchangeably, for both the fiber and wool content disclosures with wool having one additional option for when it can be used. It is permissible to use either "All" or "100%" when the textile or wool product is wholly or partially of one fiber, e.g., "100% Cotton," or where a portion of the article is all one fiber. Additionally, in the case of a wool product that is wholly of one fiber except for the inclusion of any fiber ornamentation that does not exceed 5 percent, "All" or "100%" may be used provided the correct generic fiber names, and any necessary qualifying phrase if needed, is included. For example:

- 100% Wool—Exclusive of Decoration

Use of term "virgin" and "new"[39]

The fiber content disclosure of a textile fiber product can only include the term "virgin" or "new" where such fiber had never been reclaimed from any spun, woven, knitted, felted, bonded, or similarly manufactured product. Such is the case whether the description pertains to the entire article or to a part of it. Similarly, the wool rules disallow use of these terms when the product is not 100 percent composed of new or virgin fibers.

Country of origin identification

The country of origin identification on wearing apparel is subject to two different sets of laws. The first are those of the FTC and the second are those of US Customs and Border Protection (CBP) which are applicable to all imported merchandise. The FTC requires a disclosure of the name of the country where the imported product was processed or manufactured.[40] In order to promote consistency between determinations made by CBP and the FTC about a product's origin, the FTC amended its rules in 2014 to state that an imported product's country of origin shall be that as determined by the laws of CBP, which are discussed more fully in Chapter 6.[41]

Made in USA[42]

When made in the USA, each textile fiber and wool product completely made in America of US originating materials must be labeled using the term "Made in USA" or some other clear and equivalent term. When made either in whole or in part of imported materials, a label disclosing these facts is required, for example, "Made in USA of Imported Fabric" or, "Knitted in USA of Imported Yarn." Labels on products partially manufactured in a foreign country and partially made in the US must indicate the same, for example, "U.S.A. Components Assembled in Mexico."[43]

Where imported items will be subject to further manufacturing, origin is based upon such activity that is one step removed from their manufacturing process. For example, a yarn manufacturer must identify the country from which the yarn's fibers were imported, a cloth manufacturer that of the imported yarn, and a product manufacturer that of imported cloth or yarns for products made directly from such yarn.

Additional rules for garments containing a neck

Garments with a neck are mandated to have the label disclosing the country of origin at the inside center of the neck midway between the shoulder seams, or in close proximity to another label affixed to the inside center of the neck, and the disclosure must appear on the front of a label.[44] It should be noted that the country of origin is the only disclosure that requires appearing on the front of a label in a specific location.

Registered Identification Number[45]

A "Registered Identification Number," which is commonly referred to as an "RN#," is an available alternative to the usage of a company's name that is doing business.[46] The process for obtaining one is consistent across the TFPIA, WPLA, and FPLA and may be placed on a label instead of the company name. An RN# can only be used by the company to whom it is issued, and such numbers are not transferable or assignable.[47] It will be subject to cancellation where deemed necessary in the public interest, where the prompt notification of any change in name, business address, or legal business status of a person or firm to whom an RN# has been assigned is not made to the FTC, or where it is discovered that it had been obtained for deceptive purposes. Any person residing in the US can create an account and apply for an RN# online at http://www.ftc.gov.

Using a substitute label to identify the actual RN# holder[48]

Substituting a label will be necessary where the identity of a company has changed due to a textile product changing "ownership," for example where the product gets incorporated into a new article that is sold by a different entity, or the original is resold by another seller. Substitute labels are allowed where, for example, there is a change in who the seller is, as the actual RN# holder should be indicated on a label in order to truthfully identify such party. When necessary to avoid deception, the name of any person other than the manufacturer of the product appearing on the label affixed to such product must be accompanied by appropriate words showing that the product was not manufactured by such person, for example "Manufactured for: _____, Distributed by: _____."

The care labeling rule[49]

A **care label** states what regular care is needed for the ordinary use of a product, which for wearing apparel specifically means having either a washing or dry-cleaning instruction.[50] While either method can be used, the label needs to have only one method stated and have a reasonable basis for recommending such care of the article.[51] Manufacturers and importers of textile wearing apparel and certain piece goods such as a bolt of fabric, or anyone responsible for instructing these parties, must ensure that regular care instructions are provided at the time such products are sold to purchasers.[52] The information must be easily seen or found and where it is packaged, folded, or displayed in a way that renders it hard to find, the care information must also appear on the outside of the package or on a hang tag fastened to the product.[53] Washing information must state an appropriate water temperature or indicate if it should be washed by hand.[54] An

Figure 2.3 Care label instructions prominently placed along the neckline of a t-shirt. Source: Deanna Clark-Esposito.

appropriate drying and ironing temperature must also be disclosed, as should any bleaching or other appropriate warnings, such as "do not bleach," as illustrated in Figure 2.3.

Where dry cleaning instructions are provided, they must state at least one type of solvent that may be used unless all commercially available types of solvent can be used, in which case no specification is necessary. Where any part of the dry cleaning procedure or any other washing procedure can reasonably be expected to harm the product or others being cleaned with it, however, the label must contain a warning to this effect and include the words "Do Not," "No," "Only," or some other clear wording, such as the "Do Not Bleach" warning in Figure 2.3.

ASTMs Standard Guide for Care Symbols

The symbols founds in the ASTM International Standard publication number ASTM-D5489 entitled, "Standard Guide for Care Symbols for Care Instructions on Textile Products (ASTM D5489)" may be used on care of labels or care instructions in lieu of the terms. A copy of ASTM D5489 may be purchased via the ASTM website at www.astm.org.[55]

Special issues when dealing with fur products

Products containing fur are considerably more complicated to deal in due to additional international trade laws that must be abided by (see Chapter 6), and the adherence to specific labeling laws under the FPLA. While the FPLA contains an entire body of law dedicated to how fur products are labeled, which are only marginally covered in this book, the following discusses how to reference fur names when labeling products subject to the TFPIA and WPLA laws and their regulations.

Using fur-bearing animal names and symbols[56]

While there are no WPLA rules specific to using fur-bearing animal names and symbols, there are several in relation to textile fiber products. As long as the name is not prohibited for use by the FPLA, where a garment or other textile fiber product contains 5 percent or more of the hair or fiber of a fur-bearing animal, the name of the animal may be used in the fiber disclosure, provided the name of such animal is used in conjunction with the words "fiber," "hair," or "blend," e.g., "80 percent Rabbit hair, 20 percent Nylon."[57] Unless actually present in the article however, any word or name symbolic of a fur-bearing animal by reason of conventional usage, or its close relationship with fur-bearing animals, is prohibited and should therefore not be used in a disclosure.

Use of terms mohair, cashmere and "fur" fibers[58]

Labels on products containing hair of the Angora goat known as "mohair," or containing hair or fleece of the Cashmere goat known as "cashmere," may state the term "mohair" or "cashmere" in lieu of the word "wool," together with its respective percentage of each such fiber, for example, "60% Cotton—40% Recycled Cashmere." If used, it must be done so consistently, whether included as Required Information or for other purposes. In addition, where there are any depictions connoting or implying their presence, the disclosed fiber content must also contain the word "mohair" or "cashmere."

Violations, enforcement and penalties for non-compliance

The basic consumer protection statute enforced by the FTC provides that "unfair or deceptive acts or practices in or affecting commerce . . . are . . . declared unlawful."[59] To this end, many of the errors that can occur with improper labeling result in "misbranding," which occurs when Required Information is not properly or sufficiently disclosed.[60] It is a violation of the TFPIA, WPLA, and FPLA to manufacture, distribute, transport or deliver for shipment, sell or offer for sale, or advertise any misbranded product.[61] When this or any other violation of the law occurs, a violator can face a penalty or other enforcement action by the FTC.

Misbranding

Misbranding encompasses a broad range of labeling errors, including those not properly labeled, stamped, tagged or marked, but also where the text of any Required Information is minimized, rendered obscure or inconspicuous, or is placed in a way likely to be unnoticed or unseen by purchasers when the product is offered or displayed for sale, or sold to purchasers.[62] Being "unseen" can also occur by using small or indistinct type, a failure to use letters and numerals of equal size in naming all fibers and percentages of such fibers, having an insufficient background contrast, or via crowding, intermingling, or obscuring the designs, vignettes, or other written, printed or graphic matter. Where the care label information is missing, that is also a violation as it is considered by the FTC to be a deceptive act or practice.[63] This is the case regardless of the intent and irrespective of whether it resulted from willfulness or negligence.[64] As the general law governing misbranding applies to so many types of "unfair or deceptive acts or practices," multiple violations may be alleged against a single misbranded label.

Recordkeeping requirements[65]

Recordkeeping is a very important aspect of compliance and the requirement to retain records applies to a fur, textile fiber, or wool product manufacturer (or such importer or other person that instructs a manufacturer) in relation to the fiber content of all products made, the country in which the product was made or the wool processed or manufactured, the name or RN# of the manufacturer (or other relevant party), as well as anyone that has substituted an original label from a product they are selling with respect to the information removed. The maintenance of records is required so that a traceable line of continuity, from raw materials through processing to the finished product, can readily be determined for reasons such as in the event of a product recall. Records are required to be preserved for at least three years and to neglect or refuse to maintain or preserve these records is considered unlawful and can lead to an allegation of engaging in an unfair method of competition, and an unfair or deceptive act or practice, which ultimately, can lead to penalties.[66]

Penalties

Penalty amounts are subject to change in accordance with inflation, and substantial increases went into effect on August 1, 2016 from what had formerly been the maximum penalty amounts across a variety of violations.[67] Examples include an increase from $210 to $525 per day for a violation of failing to maintain the required records under the WPLA, and for that of misbranding, an increase from $16,000 per violation to $40,000. Clearly, the FTC is sending a signal to those selling fashion merchandise of the importance to exercise due diligence in their product compliance protocols.

To avoid an allegation of misbranding, the person charged must prove that the entire deviation or variation from the fiber content percentages stated on the label resulted from unavoidable variations in its manufacture and occurred despite the exercise of due care, e.g., via lab tests of the raw materials preproduction for a fiber content declaration that provided the basis for any label disclosures. Such had not been proven by several retailers in 2013 who were collectively penalized $1.26 million for labeling products as "bamboo" when they were, according to the FTC, rayon. As explained in the case study below, it does not pay to make statements that are misleading in an effort to attract a certain type of customer.

Resources for more information

- *Threading Your Way Through the Labeling Requirements Under the Textile and Wool Acts.*[68] https://www.ftc.gov/tips-advice/business-center/guidance/ threading-your-way-through-labeling-requirements-under-textile

- *Clothes Captioning: Complying with the Care Labeling Rule.*[69] https://www.ftc. gov/tips-advice/business-center/guidance/clothes-captioning-complying-care-labeling-rule

Key terms

care label	label, labeled, and	textile fiber product
elastic	labeling	wearing apparel
fabric	misbranding	wool
fiber	ornamentation	wool product
household textile articles	recycled wool	
interlining	remnant	

Discussion questions and exercises

1 Under the TFPIA rules, when must a fiber of less than 5 percent of the total fiber weight of a product be disclosed?

2 What is the difference between how the TFPIA and WPLA require disclosures of fibers that are less than 5 percent of the total fiber weight of the product?

3 Will a product labeler be subject to a violation of misbranding for disclosing a sweater was composed of 38 percent recycled wool when it was made up, in fact, of 35 percent recycled wool?

4 If you had a trademarked fiber called "Bio-Fabrica USA" which was made up of the generic fibers cotton and viscose, how would you prepare a lawful label that included the disclosure "Bio-Fabrica USA" on it? Draw the sample label containing the fiber content disclosure.

Case study Experienced retailers get hit with penalties for misleading bamboo claims[70]

It is commonly perceived that the large retailers are aware of what their compliance protocols are with respect to the labeling of wearing apparel. Unfortunately, in an effort to attract eco-conscious consumers, five of them violated the FTCs textile laws related to misbranding and faced a cumulative $1.26 million dollar penalty alleging their

---

textiles were made of bamboo when they were actually made of rayon. Specifically, the retailers and their penalties were: Amazon.com, Inc. $455,000; Leon Max, Inc. $80,000; Sears Roebuck and Co. $475,000; Macys, Inc. $250,000.

From clothing to bed sheets, the FTC decided that the retailers knew or should have known that these mislabeled products were not made of bamboo and yet despite this, disclosed this fiber as the Required Information. To make matters worse, they had been sent a "Warning Letter" from the FTC that specifically noted not merely the relevant laws pertaining to compliance with the TFPIA—which the retailers were subject to—but also that it was an unfair or deceptive act or practice to falsely or deceptively stamp, tag, label, invoice, advertise, or otherwise identify any textile fiber product regarding the name or amount of constituent fibers contained therein. The FTC further reminded them of the civil penalties that must be assessed where a violation has been found. Despite this, the retailers continued to market and sell the rayon textile products advertised and labeled as bamboo. They were all ultimately found to be in violation of misbranding due to these false and/or deceptively labeled products, as to both the name and/or amount of the constituent fibers, and were found to have done so with knowledge. They were therefore penalized accordingly.

Notes

1. 16 CFR §303.16; 16 CFR §300.5; 16 CFR §301.20.
2. 16 CFR §303.1.
3. Ibid.
4. Ibid.
5. Ibid.
6. 16 CFR §303.4; 16 CFR §300.7.
7. Ibid.
8. 16 CFR §303.15.
9. 16 CFR §303.28; 16 CFR §303.29.
10. 16 CFR §300.12.
11. Ibid.
12. 16 CFR §303.45.

13. http://www.iso.org/iso/home/store/catalogue_ics/catalogue_detail_ics.htm?csnumber
    =56206 (viewed on July 28, 2016).
14. 16 CFR §303.6; 16 CFR §300.8(a).
15. Ibid.
16. 16 CFR §303.17; 16 CFR §300.8(c)–(f).
17. 79 FR 32157, 32160 (06/04/14).
18. Ibid.
19. 16 CFR §303.16; 16 CFR §303.3(a).
20. 16 CFR §303.25; 16 § CFR 300.22.
21. 16 CFR §303.43.
22. 16 CFR §303.24.
23. 16 CFR §300.29.
24. 16 CFR §303.14.
25. Ibid.
26. 16 CFR §303.13; 15 USC §70b(f).
27. 16 CFR §300.21; 16 CFR §303.21.
28. 16 CFR §303.31.
29. 16 CFR §303.26.
30. Ibid.
31. 16 CFR §303.12.
32. Ibid.
33. 16 CFR §303.22.
34. Ibid.
35. 16 CFR §303.45.
36. 16 CFR §303.45(a).
37. 16 CFR §303.3.
38. 16 CFR §303.27; 16 CFR §300.17.
39. 16 CFR §303.35; 16 CFR §300.20.
40. 15 U.S.C. § 70b(b); 15 U.S.C. § 68b(d).
41. 79 FR 32157, 32164 (06/04/14); 79 FR 18766, 18771 (04/04/14).
42. 16 CFR §303.33.
43. Ibid.
44. 16 CFR §303.15(b).
45. 16 CFR §300.4; 16 CFR §303.20.
46. 16 CFR §300.13.
47. 16 CFR §300.4.
48. 16 CFR §300.14; 15 USC §70c(b).
49. 16 CFR Part 423.
50. 16 CFR §423.6.
51. 16 CFR §423.6(b).

52. 16 CFR §423.3.

53. 16 CFR §423.6(a).

54. 16 CFR §423.6.

55. https://www.astm.org/Standards/D5489.htm (viewed on July 31, 2016).

56. 16 CFR §303.9.

57. 16 CFR §303.6.

58. 16 CFR §300.19; 79 FR 32157, 32163 (06/04/14).

59. 15 U.S.C. §45(a)(1).

60. 15 U.S.C. §68d; 15 U.S.C. §70e.

61. 15 U.S.C. §68a; 15 U.S.C. §70a.

62. 16 CFR §300.11 and §300.30.

63. 16 CFR §423.5.

64. In re Smithline Coats Co., 45 FTC 79 (1948).

65. 16 CFR §300.31; 15 USC §68d(b); 15 USC §70d.

66. 15 U.S.C. §41 et seq.

67. 81 FR 42476 (06/30/16).

68. https://www.ftc.gov/tips-advice/business-center/guidance/threading-your-way-through-labeling-requirements-under-textile (viewed on July 10, 2016).

69. https://www.ftc.gov/tips-advice/business-center/guidance/clothes-captioning-complying-care-labeling-rule (viewed on July 10, 2016).

70. https://www.ftc.gov/enforcement/cases-proceedings/102–3127/sears-roebuck-co-kmart-corporation-kmartcom-llc-united-states (viewed on August 2, 2016) (Sears Roebuck); https://www.ftc.gov/enforcement/cases-proceedings/102–3129/macys-inc-united-states-america-federal-trade-commission (viewed on August 2, 2016) (Macys); https://www.ftc.gov/enforcement/cases-proceedings/102–3126/leon-max-inc-also-dba-max-studio (viewed on August 2, 2016) (Leon Max); https://www.ftc.gov/enforcement/cases-proceedings/102–3132/amazoncom-inc-united-states-america-federal-trade-commission (viewed on August 2, 2016) (Amazon).

Chapter 3

Intellectual property: Protection, enforcement and hidden issues

The rise of coverage by mainstream media of court cases involving allegations of intellectual property (IP) rights violations has resulted in increased anxiety levels amongst both established fashion brands and new designers alike. While some of it is warranted, it raises the question as to just how much legal protection is available given the nature of clothing, whose very purpose is often times considered simply utilitarian, rather than artistic.

Learning objectives

- Distinguish the types of intellectual property that the fashion industry relies on for protection
- Understand the process of filing for a trademark or copyright registration
- Describe the global mechanisms available for IP protection
- Understand US Customs' role in protecting IP at the border

While the lengths to which IP protection should extend over the fashion industry may be left to the courts to answer, it can be said that there are several facets of the industry as a whole that are in need of protection. They range from a product design or functionality standpoint, to issues involving the manufacture of counterfeit goods, which have been linked to child and slave labor, as well as that such sales have been connected to the funding of terrorist activities.

Protecting intellectual property in the US

Many financial benefits flow to the owner of intellectual property as it is an asset and therefore has a monetary value. The term intellectual property generally

---

Box 3.1 Intellectual property protection in the US

US federal government agency	Types of IP it protects
US Patent and Trademark Office (USPTO): www.uspto.gov	• Trademarks • Patents
US Copyright Office: www.copyright.gov	• Copyrights

---

refers to creations of the mind that are creative works or ideas embodied in a shareable form which can enable others to re-create, emulate, or manufacture them.[1] In order to maintain and not diminish the value of IP, it is important to monitor and prevent its unauthorized use. Doing so prevents the diminishing of a brand through the sale of products of a lower quality as well as for ensuring the owner's exclusive right to capitalize on the proceeds from such IP. One step for preventing the unauthorized use of IP is to have it recognized as being your own property. This is done by obtaining its lawful registration through the appropriate federal government agency (Box 3.1), be it a copyright, trademark, or patent, each of which is described in detail in this chapter.

While some state governments provide an avenue for IP registration, it is limited in that any protective reach extends only as far as the boundaries of that particular state. For this reason it is recommended to register at the federal agency level (Box 3.1) so that protective coverage may be obtained nationwide.

Copyright protection and the fashion industry

Copyright protects an original work of authorship fixed in any tangible medium of expression from which such work can be either directly perceived, reproduced, or otherwise communicated, or done so with the aid of a machine or device.[2] Its protection extends to the variety of works listed in Box 3.2 and is an applicable form of protection for several types of activities within the fashion industry, including photographs from a photo shoot, music made to accompany a fashion show, and the filmed recording of the fashion show itself.

Copyright protection typically does not extend to clothing

Despite all of the available protections (Box 3.2), for more than seventy-five years it has been settled in the courts of the US that articles of clothing are

Box 3.2 Types of copyrights[3]

Pictorial, graphic, and sculptural works

Literary works

Musical works, including any accompanying words

Dramatic works, including any accompanying music

Motion pictures and other audiovisual works

Architectural works

Sound recordings

Pantomimes and choreographic works

"useful articles" not protected by the Copyright Act.[4] This is because the courts have ruled that copyright protection is only extended to the design elements of clothing in such instances where those elements, individually or together, are **separable**, that is, where they are "physically or conceptually" separate from the garment itself.[5] Moreover, because physical separability can only be shown where one or more decorative elements "can actually be removed from the original item and separately sold, without adversely impacting the article's functionality," it is a high bar for most articles of clothing to successfully surmount.[6]

What copyright registration gives you

Registration with the US Copyright Office is simple to do and once it has been obtained, the owner of a protected work has an exclusive right to use it.[7] This means they have the right to manufacture products embodying its design, to instruct foreign manufacturers to do so, and to lawfully import such products.[8] Importantly, by owning a registered copyright, an ability to prevent others from using it now exists, and copyright protection provides several other economic benefits with respect to enforcing such rights in a court of law that would not be available for recovery in a lawsuit without the registration. For these reasons, it is encouraged that registration be done as soon as possible and the format of a copyright notice to indicate ownership should be made in the following style: © 2018. DCEsposito Corp., All Rights Reserved.

Copyright protection commences at the moment of the creation of a work until seventy years after the author's death.[9] Where a work is a **work for hire**, which is a "copyrightable work produced either by an employee within the scope of employment or by an independent contractor under a written agreement"[10] and is therefore owned by a corporation, the copyright duration is extended to ninety-five years after publication or 120 years after creation, whichever comes first.[11]

Copyright filing and resources

The US Copyright's website is www.copyright.gov and an application for a copyright registration can be obtained and filed electronically there. The cost for such filing is $35 when done online or $55 when submitted by mail. The website contains several publications to help registrants make sense of available protections, protocols, and instructions on how to file.

It should be noted that a filing made with the US Copyright Office affords protection against unauthorized use within the US only, and would not extend to other countries. Many countries, including the US, however, are members of an international treaty known as the Berne Convention, which recognizes the rights of copyright owners in each member country and extends to them the same protection as that which would be afforded to a national citizen who registered in their home country.

Trademarks

Commonly referred to as The Lanham Act, the Trademark Act of 1946[12] is a US federal law that gives a producer or a seller the exclusive right to "register" a trademark and to prevent its competitors from using it.[13] A **trademark** is "any word, name, symbol, design, or any combination thereof, used in commerce to identify and distinguish the goods of one manufacturer or seller from those of another and to indicate the source of the goods"—even if the source is unknown.[14]

Secondary meaning

While an applicant may be capable of obtaining a trademark for a color, in order to successfully obtain one it requires that a person use or intend to use the mark to identify and distinguish a brand from other sellers' products so that over time customers come to recognize a particular color on a product or its packaging as signifying a specific brand. In so doing, this color would indicate its source or otherwise identify and distinguish the goods, much in the way that descriptive words on a product can come to indicate a product's origin. When this happens, a **secondary meaning** is found to have occurred, which is when "in the minds of the public, the primary significance of a product feature ... is to identify the source of the product rather than the product itself."[15] A recent example confirming this longstanding position of the law was reflected in the court case of *Christian Louboutin S.A. v. Yves Saint Laurent America Holdings, Inc.*[16] In this case, Yves Saint Laurent® (YSL) designed and sold high-heeled shoes with the bright red sole recognized as characteristic of the Christian Louboutin® brand. Having acquired a secondary meaning on its red-soled shoe, the court's decision—which ruled in Louboutin's favor—reiterated that a color can enjoy trademark protections once such a feature has created the identification of the source of the product (in this case Louboutin) rather than the product itself.[17]

A product must be used "in commerce"

The power of the federal government to register a mark derives from the Commerce Clause of the US Constitution and Section 1 of the Lanham Act.[18] This law specifically authorizes the making of an application for the registration of "a trademark used in commerce"[19] or alternatively, to submit an application where a person has a bona fide intention to use a trademark in commerce.[20] **Commerce** is defined under the Lanham Act as "all commerce which may lawfully be regulated by Congress," and defines **use in commerce** as "the bona fide use of a mark in the ordinary course of trade, and not made merely to reserve a right in a mark."[21] A trademark is recognized as being used *in commerce* when it is placed in any manner on a good, its container, any displays associated with it, or on the tags or labels affixed to it, and sold or transported in commerce.[22] In the event the nature of the goods makes such placement impracticable, then placing such a mark on documents associated with the goods or their sale is considered sufficient.[23]

The service mark

A **service mark** can also be registered with the USPTO for protection. It is any word, name, symbol, or device, or any combination thereof either used by a person, or for which a person has a bona fide intention to use in commerce such word, name, etc. to identify and distinguish the services of one person or entity from the services of others, and to indicate the source of the services.[24]

Similar to that of a trademark, a service mark is considered used *in commerce* when it is used or displayed in the sale or advertising of services, and when such services are actually rendered in commerce, including where rendered in more than one state, or in both the United States and a foreign country.[25]

Protection and USPTO registration

The US Patent and Trademark Office (USPTO) is the federal agency that registers trademarks and service marks, and also grants US patents, as discussed later in this chapter. Through this office various types of IP may be protected, including designs, patterns, formulas, business names, logos, and more. Its website at www.uspto.gov provides more than just a portal for submitting the application for a registration, it also includes several resources for learning about trademarks and patents, details on how to maintain your registration, and explains the global systems available for international protection.

Trademark protections attained through USPTO registration

Benefits to obtaining a USPTO registration include that it

1 establishes the validity of the registrant's ownership;
2 provides protection as of the date of the application;
3 provides potential competitors with notice as to the existence of rights by the trademark holder; and
4 after five years of continuous use, USPTO registration also renders the mark incontestable.[26]

These protective benefits would not extend to an unregistered trademark. Rather, its coverage would be limited to the protections afforded by common law trademark rights and protection under Section 43(a) of the Lanham Act, which protects a mark against false designations of origin and false descriptions.[27]

Indicating the existence of a trademark or service mark

Prior to obtaining a registration from USPTO, a product should be marked with "TM" for a trademark and "SM" for a service mark. Once obtained, the use of the ® symbol may follow such protected mark to indicate such rights exist.[28]

Classes of goods and services

Whether in relation to a trademark or service mark, an application to register the mark must be filed, i.e. submitted, to the USPTO providing written details about the property itself, renderings and other technical drawings that depict it, and the payment of a registration fee, commonly referred to as the "filing fee."[29]

Protection is limited in the sense that an applicant may only file an application for protection within the categories of goods and services as they are actually currently being used in commerce. Registration is segmented into a "class system" and when filing to obtain a mark, a registrant must specify the classes that actually apply to the sales channels, i.e. the use in commerce, for which the product is being sold in. Comprised of forty-five classes in all, the categories range from chemicals in Class 1, to specific personal and social services in Class 45, with the primary categories for fashion merchandise, falling into the following classes:

Class 14: Jewelry and precious metals

Class 18: Leather and imitation leather goods

Class 23: Yarns and threads for textile use

Class 24: Fabrics, blankets, covers, and textiles

Class 25: Clothing, footwear and headgear

Class 26: Lace, embroidery, ribbons, buttons, braids.

A separate registration fee is required for each class of goods the registration of a mark is sought. While there are circumstances that warrant a reduction in filing fees, the cost for a regular application is $325 per class of good or service.[30] For example, a registrant may apply to have a mark used for goods in two classes, such as for t-shirts in Class 25 and leather bags in Class 18. In this case, they would be obligated to pay for two classes, or $650.

It is important to remember that the protection afforded by trademark registration is only valid for those categories of goods or services that have been applied for and actually obtained. Where protection covering an additional product type is sought, a new trademark application would need to be filed for coverage of those goods in the other classes.

Intent to use application

Where a product is about to be offered in commerce, but has yet to have done so, an application may be filed under an **intent-to-use** basis, which means the applicant has a bona fide intention to use such mark on their goods or services they are, or planning, to sell.[31] Once the mark is being used and sold in commerce, a separate application may be filed to actually register the trademark with USPTO.

Pre-registration considerations

As explained by trademark attorney Laurie Marshall in the case study at the end of this chapter, attention must be paid to having a comprehensive search of a mark's use in commerce in advance of both using it, and filing a trademark application for such mark, in order to avoid the costs and headaches that accompany an allegation of unauthorized trademark use. Where such abuse is discovered, a "cease and desist" letter may be sent by the trademark holder demanding that the unauthorized use be immediately terminated, and where it is not stopped, action involving the courts may ensue.

Maintaining trademark rights after you have obtained them

When it comes to a trademark, obtaining the registration is just one step to protecting a holder's rights as the opportunity to ensure such exclusive ongoing use of the registered trademark hinges, in part, on one's ability to monitor the marketplace for use by potential infringers and where found, to demand such use of it be stopped.[32] This remains an ongoing obligation placed on a trademark holder for the life of the mark where the exclusive use of it is desired.

USPTO also requires that between the fifth and sixth year after registration, use of the mark be demonstrated by filing an affirmation that it is still in use, and a failure to do so will result in the cancelation of the mark.[33] In addition, a renewal for the trademark must be done on the ten year anniversary, and thereafter, once every ten years a renewal must be filed.[34]

The legal standard for trademark enforcement

An extensive framework for regulating the use of trademarks and protecting them against infringement, dilution, and unfair competition exists under the Lanham Act.[35] The parameters for successfully commencing a lawsuit of an infringement claim is likewise comprehensive, in that the **plaintiff**, who is the party that starts a lawsuit, must prove (1) that they have a valid, protectable trademark, and (2) that the **defendant**, the party against whom the plaintiff's claims are made, has a product or service in common with the plaintiff's that is likely to cause consumer confusion,[36] or that customers could mistake, or be deceived as to, the source of the product.[37] In addition, an essential inquiry made with this type of a case is whether a reasonably prudent customer in the marketplace could likely have been confused as to the origin of the good or service bearing one of the marks, due to the similarities that exist between the two of them.[38]

The difference between a "counterfeit" and a "knockoff" good

Whether referred to as a "counterfeit" or a "knock off," stories about **infringing goods**, that is, such merchandise which is using the intellectual property of another without authorization to do so, are regularly heard of in the news today. **Counterfeit goods** are those intending to be passed off as the original article itself in that they possess a **counterfeit mark**, which is a spurious designation which is identical with, or substantially indistinguishable from, a registered mark.[39] A **knock off** on the other hand, is a virtual replica of the original article, which for example, though it may be made of inferior quality materials, is nonetheless similar enough to create consumer confusion in the marketplace.[40]

The trade dress category

Trade dress refers to the image and overall appearance or presentation of a product, such as that of the shape of the footwear shown in Figure 3.1 that is akin to footwear manufactured under the Crocs® brand.[41]

It can also refer to a product's configuration and or packaging.[42] While trade dress is protected under the Lanham Act, where a trade dress infringement claim is made pursuant to it, the plaintiff must successfully show that its trade dress is protectable and that the defendant's use of the trade dress is likely to cause consumer confusion.[43]

Obtaining patent protection

To understand the concept of a patent it is easiest to begin with an example. Using two approved footwear patents, attorney Kristin Grant (in Box 3.3) explains the benefits that derive from obtaining either a design or utility patent, in addition to explaining the concept of having the "freedom to operate."

Figure 3.1 Footwear with an appearance similar to the Crocs® brand of shoes. Source: Deanna Clark-Esposito.

Box 3.3 Patent protection for the fashion industry by Kristin Grant of Grant Attorneys at Law, PLLC

A patent provides an inventor or an assignee with the right to exclude others from making, using, offering for sale, selling or importing an invention without permission, during the term of the patent.[44] While a patent is a potentially lucrative asset, the length of time and cost to obtain it may make it impractical for some in an industry driven by seasonal trends. Patent protection is more practical in fashion when sought for articles such as wearable technology, functional fabrics, manufacturing processes, and products or features of products with a longer lifespan. Two types of patents relevant to the fashion industry, which are available under US law, are design patents and utility patents.

Design patents
Design patent protection is available for the ornamental features of a useful article and typically covers the shape of a product and its surface

ornamentation. A design patent issued from an application filed on or after May 13, 2015, remains in effect for a term of fifteen years from the date of grant.[45] In order to obtain design patent protection, the claimed design must be new, non-obvious and applied to a useful article.[46]

Design patents have become increasingly popular in the fashion industry as a method of enforcement against knock offs, allowing designers or their assignees to obtain a monopoly over specific features of an article. Fashion related articles for which design patent protection is commonly sought include handbags, jewelry, footwear, eyeglasses, and perfume bottles. The example in Figure 3.2 shows a drawing sheet of the US design patent with patent number US D599,986 covering the design of a shoe sole.

Where design patents are concerned, protection extends only to those features which are illustrated in the drawings. Elements represented by broken lines typically represent the environment surrounding what is being claimed and do not form claimed features of the invention. Therefore, protection does not apply to those elements. In this example, the body of the shoe is represented by broken lines and is thus not a claimed feature of the invention. What this means is that a third party who applies this sole design to any shoe body

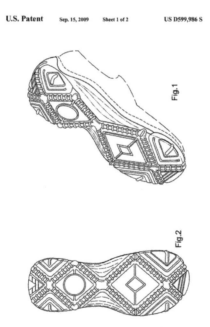

U.S. Patent   Sep. 15, 2009   Sheet 1 of 2   US D599,986 S

Fig.1

Fig.2

Figure 3.2 US design patent of shoe sole. Source: United States Patent and Trademark Office.

would likely be liable for patent infringement. If the application only claimed design rights to the shoe as a whole (i.e., the body was also represented in solid lines in all drawings), then it would be increasingly difficult to enforce the patent against designs with a starkly different shoe body. For this reason, it is important to include variations in the drawings claiming both broad and narrow protection so as to ensure maximum protection against potential infringers.

Utility patents

Utility patent protection is available for the structure and function of an invention which is novel, useful, and non-obvious.[47] Lasting for twenty years from the earliest application filing date,[48] utility patents are ideal for articles which have unique functionalities and structures. Examples of fashion related items for which utility patent protection may be sought include a method of making a type of fabric, a compression garment, and a smart watch. The example in Figure 3.3 shows a drawing sheet of a US utility patent (No. 6,505,424) assigned to Mizumo Corporation, covering the structure of an athletic shoe.

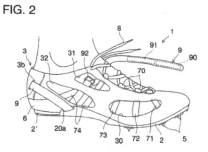

U.S. Patent   Jan. 14, 2003   Sheet 1 of 7   US 6,505,424 B2

FIG. 1

FIG. 2

Figure 3.3 Drawing sheet of US utility patent for athletic shoe. Source: United States Patent and Trademark Office.

In this example, the invention claims a lightweight running shoe with a novel structure providing a reduction in air resistance. In contrast to design patent drawings, and as seen here, utility patent drawings include number or letter labels which correspond to the features of the article as described in the detailed description section of the patent.

In a utility patent, protection extends only to those features which are laid out in the claims section of the patent. The example in Figure 3.4 shows a drawing sheet of a US utility patent (No. 7,618,260) covering a wearable modular interface strap.

U.S. Patent   Nov. 17, 2009   Sheet 1 of 18   US 7,618,260 B2

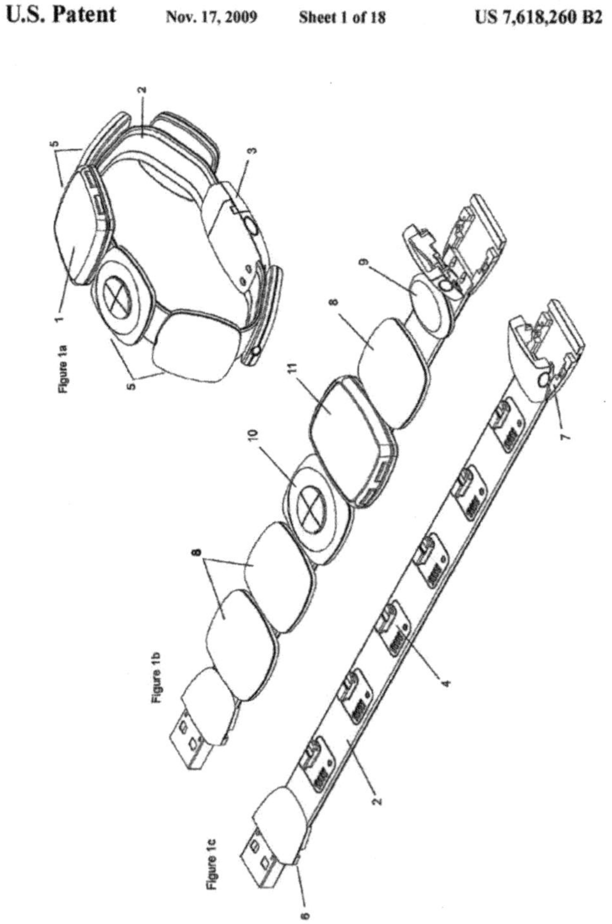

Figure 3.4 Drawing sheet of US utility patent for wearable modular interface strap. Source: United States Patent and Trademark Office.

> While the claims define the limits of what the inventor or assignee has rights to, the USPTO gives them their broadest reasonable interpretation in light of the specification.[49]
>
> ### Freedom to operate
>
> Designers tend to draw inspiration from pre-existing sources and are continuously recycling past trends. While patent protection can add value when applied to the right product, another important consideration is avoiding infringement of another party's patent. The process of determining this potential risk of infringement is coined **freedom to operate**. A freedom to operate search consists of a search of prior patents and published patent applications to determine whether the commercialization of an article may be infringing on a third party's rights. This is a useful tool when developing new products and may be worthwhile for reducing the potential risk of liability.

Global intellectual property protection

In an effort to create a balanced and effective system of global intellectual property, the World Intellectual Property Organization (WIPO) was created. It publishes the *International Classification of Goods and Services for the Purposes of the Registration of Marks* which enables a uniform global process to identify a good or service based on a numerical code, and supports the streamlining of international trademark registration on a global basis.[50]

International trademark registration

On December 1, 1995, the Protocol Relating to the Madrid Agreement Concerning the International Registration of Marks came into existence and the US came to recognize and follow it in 2003. Commonly referred to as the Madrid Protocol, it provides for the registration of a trademark in several countries through a single filing with WIPO for its global protection. The application for the international registration has the same effect as a national application would have in each of the countries designated by an applicant and once protection is granted, the mark is afforded protection in each of those jurisdictions as if that country's national agency had registered it.[51]

International patent classification

A worldwide classification system for patents known as, the International Patent Classification (IPC), provides a global program for patent recognition. Its purpose is to provide a single platform for the common classification, research, and maintenance of published patent applications, inventors' certificates, utility models, and utility certificates.[52] Accessible through WIPO, it is a series of symbols whose meaning is understood irrespective and independent of language, and the platform enables the retrieval of patent documents on a global basis when performing a search.[53] Classifications are broadly categorized to encompass all types of merchandise. Those on textiles products have their own section and organizes articles by specifically breaking out textile types according to their fiber content, yarns, and other factors.[54]

The Paris Convention for the Protection of Industrial Property

In terms of international legal protection for patents, the Paris Convention for the Protection of Industrial Property (Paris Convention) provides for the right of an applicant of a patent or trademark to apply for protection in all the other member countries through a single application.[55] It should be noted however, that under US law a patent must first be attained from USPTO before making an application for one in a foreign country, including that under the Paris Convention.[56]

Additional IP protection through registration with US Customs

According to a report by the US Trade Representative's Office, the international trade in "counterfeit and pirated merchandise often fuels cross-border organized criminal networks" and IP infringement.[57] These activities can:

1 Trigger financial losses for rights holders and legitimate businesses.
2 Undermine the comparative advantage of the US in innovation and creativity to the detriment of American businesses and workers.
3 Endanger the public and pose risks to consumer health and safety.[58]

Infringers also generally disregard basic standards for worker health and safety and product quality and performance.[59] For these persons and others, IP rights and their protection is an issue taken very seriously in America and protecting such rights of imported products is likewise of great concern to US

Customs and Border Protection (CBP), which is the government agency with oversight of the US border as discussed more fully in Chapter 6 on imports. CBP has its own legal definition of a counterfeit trademark, which is a spurious mark identical with, or substantially indistinguishable from, a federally registered trademark.[60] CBP is mandated to look out for counterfeit merchandise imported into the US bearing marks that are registered with USPTO as the customs laws require that unauthorized imports of trademarked goods be **seized**, i.e., confiscated, absent written permission from the IP holder.[61]

Stop knock offs at the border with US Customs IP registration

While IP owners often recognize the value of registering their trademarks and copyrights with the USPTO due to the protections it affords their brands, what is lesser known and arguably underutilized, is the recording of these assets with CBP to obtain additional safeguards with respect to imported knock off and counterfeit goods. Though it does not extend to patent registrations, CBP has its own electronic system for trademark and copyright holders to record their registrations in order to protect against unauthorized importations of infringing goods. Once successfully obtained through USPTO or the US Copyright Office, a registration for IP protection must be filed through CBP itself. After completion, there are several benefits a registrant may obtain in relation to unauthorized imports, including that CBP will provide, for example when a seizure occurs, the IP registrant with the name of the manufacturer and the importer, along with a description of the merchandise, country of origin information, and the quantity seized. This enables the IP holder to perform its own investigation to identify any and all involved parties and to take action to prevent repeat offenses. Filing for CBP protection requires registering at https://iprr.cbp.gov, and a separate application must be made for each recording sought. The filing fee is $190 and once recorded, protection is good for twenty years with the effective date being that of the date the application was approved.[62]

US Customs and gray market goods

While preventing the importation of an outright counterfeit article is a relatively easy concept to grasp, a lesser known concept of a "gray market good" is another type of import that US Customs monitors. It defines restricted **gray market**

articles as "foreign-made articles bearing a genuine trademark or trade name identical with or substantially indistinguishable from one owned and recorded by a citizen of the United States or a corporation or association created or organized within the United States and imported without the authorization of the U.S. owner."[63]

CBP will protect against importations of restricted gray market articles to the extent that copyrights and trademarks of products carrying such IP have been recorded with its agency. Where CBP has conferred gray market protection, imported merchandise bearing the protected IP will be detained and is subject to potential seizure. With so much protection available at the border with CBP as a trade partner, an investment in this recordation is well worth the security.

Staying informed about intellectual property and fashion

Thanks to online forums like LinkedIn® with its Business of Fashion group and Julie Zerbo's The Fashion Law, in addition to countless other blogs and news outlets, staying abreast of issues impacting the fashion industry, including IP, has become relatively simple to do. Digital publications like *Women's Wear Daily*® and the fashion sections of popular publications like the *New York Times*®, with its many style sections in its online edition, illustrate the rise in a demonstrable interest and IP issues in the industry by the public at large. Resources for learning more on the business of fashion, including IP, may be viewed directly at the sources cited below:

- *Women's Wear Daily*: www.WWD.com
- BBC News: http://www.bbc.com/news
- *New York Times*: http://www.nytimes.com
- Bloomsbury Fashion Central: https://www.bloomsburyfashioncentral.com
- *Apparel Magazine*: http://apparel.edgl.com/home
- Retail Merchandiser: http://www.retail-merchandiser.com/
- Wearables.com: http://www.wearables.com
- Fashion Compliance: http://www.fashioncompliance.com
- Fashion United: https://fashionunited.com/news/fashion

Resources for more information

US Copyright Office: www.copyright.gov

US Patent and Trademark Office: www.uspto.gov

How US Customs can help protect intellectual property rights: https://www.cbp.gov/trade/priority-issues/ipr/protection

World Intellectual Property Organization (WIPO): www.wipo.int/portal/en

Sourcing Journal: www.sourcingjournal.com

US Trade Representative's Office: www.ustr.gov

Key terms

commerce	gray market articles	separable
copyright	infringing goods	seize
counterfeit goods	intellectual property	service mark
counterfeit mark	intent to use	trade dress
counterfeit trademark	knock off	trademark
(US Customs	patent	use in commerce
definition)	plaintiff	utility patent protection
defendant	restricted gray market	work for hire
design patent protection	articles	
freedom to operate	secondary meaning	

Discussion questions and exercises

1 For what kind of artistic works is obtaining a copyright more appropriate than a trademark?

2 Using a product of your choice, determine which class or classes of goods your product may register under for trademark protection.

3 US Customs recordation extends protection to which two types of intellectual property?

4 Explain the difference between a "counterfeit" good and a "knock off" good.

5 Explain when an IP holder would use a "cease-and-desist" letter.

Case study The importance of conducting a thorough search in advance of using or filing for a trademark, by Laurie Marshall of the Marshall Law Group

Can you explain why it is critical to have a thorough search conducted in advance of filing for a trademark and/or using a trademark that you perceive to be your own?

At every presentation, round table or networking event I attend, I am asked this very same question. This prompts me to ask the following question back:

> Does it make sense to spend thousands of dollars deciding on your business name, logo design, marketing strategy and securing social media handles, building branded sites without knowing whether they are available and will rightfully belong to you?

In order to explain why a trademark search and clearance is critical to the naming process, I first need to dispel some misconceptions about trademarks. I will then explain why going through the search and clearance process is imperative to every business owner.

All too often, business owners are misguided

Many new business owners do not understand that any word, letter, slogan, name, or design used in connection with the sale of goods or services is considered a trademark. Thus, it must be searched and cleared to determine its availability for use and registration.

Business owners often believe that having an LLC, S-Corp or other corporate identity (see Chapter 10) gives them rights to use their name on its goods and services, but it does not. The intention of an LLC, or other corporate identity, is for liability purposes and does not provide rights to use the name to identify the goods or services of the business. It is also important to note that just because the company name, domain name, twitter handle, etc. is available, does not mean the trademark will also be available.

Unfortunately, this information is not disseminated effectively enough and so many new business owners believe that their marks are available for use. All too often small businesses learn these trademark lessons the hard way.

The business owner believes that the trademark process can be done without legal guidance

The trademark clearance process requires performing a search of third-party trademarks and analyzing the search. Because the United States Patent and Trademark Office (USPTO) offers searching capabilities on its website, users tend to believe this is substantive enough to proceed with a trademark. This is untrue and the USPTO recently published the following on its website:

> WARNING: While an applicant can file his or her own trademark application . . . attorneys . . . represent most applicants. Some trademark owners may have valid and protected trademark rights that do not result from federal registration with the USPTO, and those marks may not appear in the USPTO's Trademark Electronic Search System (TESS) database. Before ever filing a trademark application, a trademark attorney can conduct a more comprehensive search for potential problems with your use of a proposed mark than you will be able to conduct in TESS. The attorney then can counsel you regarding use of the mark, recommend whether to file a trademark application, and advise you on your likelihood of success in the registration process.

Business owners are not aware of the significant and potentially devastating ramifications

Without proper due diligence, new businesses will quite often receive cease and desist letters requesting they cease all use of the trademark immediately and destroy everything bearing the trademark (products, marketing material, packaging, etc.). In many cases they will be required to provide inventory information to the opponent. This can be extremely damaging to a business, especially when it has established customer loyalty, creating the need for it to rebrand. Such action can result in huge financial losses and even lawsuits that compound the problem. Being sued in federal court for trademark infringement can exceed $200,000 in attorney fees alone.

In conclusion, remember that it is inexpensive to search, clear, and register your trademark, versus the costs associated with defending a litigation, i.e., a court case, or even responding to a cease and desist letter. When you decide to go through this process, have a qualified attorney help you assess the risks. There is no substitute for solid legal guidance.

Notes

1. https://www.uspto.gov/learning-and-resources/general-faqs#1242 (viewed on October 30, 2016).
2. *See*, 17 U.S.C. §102(a).
3. 17 U.S.C. §102(b).
4. *Jovani Fashion, Limited v. Fiesta Fashions*, Court of Appeals, 2d Cir. 2012, No. 12 – 598 – CV (citing, *Whimsicality, Inc. v. Rubie's Costume Co.*, 891 F.2d 452, 455 (2d Cir. 1989) (citing, *Fashion Originators' Guild v. FTC*, 114 F.2d 80, 84 (2d Cir. 1940) (L. Hand, J.), aff'd 312 U.S. 457 (1941)).
5. *Chosun Int'l, Inc. v. Chrisha Creations, Ltd.*, 413 F.3d 324, 328 (2d Cir. 2005).
6. *Chosun Int'l, Inc. v. Chrisha Creations, Ltd.*, 413 F.3d 324, 329 (2d Cir. 2005).
7. *See*, 17 U.S.C. §302.
8. 19 CFR §133.42.
9. 17 U.S.C. §302(a).
10. *Black's Law Dictionary*, 7th edition, West Group, p. 1600, 1999.
11. 17 U.S.C. §302(c).
12. Trademark Act of 1946 (Lanham Act), 15 U.S.C. §§1051–1127.
13. *Qualitex v. Jacobsen Products Co., Inc.*, 514 U.S. 159, 162 (1995) (citing, 15 U.S.C. §1052; §1114(1).
14. 15 U.S.C. §1127.
15. *See, Inwood Laboratories, Inc. v. Ives Laboratories, Inc.*, 456 U.S. 844, 851, n. 11 (1982).
16. *Christian Louboutin S.A. v. Yves Saint Laurent America Holdings, Inc.*, 103 U.S.P.Q.2d 1937, 696 F.3d 206 (2d Cir. 2012).
17. Ibid.
18. 15 U.S.C. §1051.
19. 15 U.S.C. §1051(a).
20. 15 U.S.C. §1051(b).
21. 15 U.S.C. §1127.
22. Ibid.

23. Ibid.

24. Ibid.

25. Ibid.

26. 15 U.S.C. §1125; 15 U.S.C. §1065.

27. 15 U.S.C. §1125.

28. http://www.inta.org/TrademarkBasics/FactSheets/Pages/TrademarkSymbolsFactSheet. aspx (viewed on June 24, 2017).

29. https://www.uspto.gov/trademark (viewed on June 24, 2017).

30. https://www.uspto.gov/learning-and-resources/fees-and-payment/uspto-fee-schedule™ Process Fee (viewed on November 13, 2016).

31. https://www.uspto.gov/trademarks-getting-started/trademark-basics/basis-filing (viewed on February 21, 2017).

32. https://www.uspto.gov/sites/default/files/documents/BasicFacts.pdf (viewed on June 24, 2017).

33. 15 U.S.C. §1065.

34. 15 U.S.C. §1059.

35. *Fortune Dynamic, Inc. v. Victoria's Secret Stores Brand Mgmt., Inc.*, 618 F.3d 1025, 1030 (9th Cir. 2010) (citing 15 U.S.C. §1051 et seq.).

36. *Adidas America, Inc. v. Skechers USA*, 149 F.Supp.3d 1222 (Dist. Ct. Or. 2016) citing, *Applied Info. Scis. Corp. v. eBay, Inc.*, 511 F.3d 966, 969 (9th Cir. 2007) (citation omitted); *Clicks Billiards, Inc. v. Sixshooters, Inc.*, 251 F.3d 1252, 1258 (9th Cir. 2001).

37. *Adidas America, Inc. v. Payless Shoe Source*, 546 F. Supp.2d 1029 (US Dist. Or. 2008) citing *Reno Air Racing Ass'n, Inc. v. McCord*, 452 F.3d 1126, 1134 (9th Cir. 2006); *Karl Storz Endoscopy-Am., Inc. v. Surgical Tech., Inc.*, 285 F.3d 848, 853–54 (9th Cir. 2002).

38. Ibid. (citing *Dreamworks Prod. Group, Inc. v. SKG Studio*, 142 F.3d 1127, 1129 (9th Cir. 1998).

39. *See*, 15 U.S.C. §1127.

40. *See generally, Diesel S.P.A. v. John Does* 1 – 9, No. 14-Civ. 4592 (S.D.N.Y. Jan. 8, 2016).

41. US Customs ruling H247145, December 27, 2013.

42. US Customs ruling HQ462025, June 20, 1996.

43. *Talking Rain Beverage Co. Inc. v. South Beach Beverage Co.*, 349 F.3d 601, 603 (9th Cir. 2003).

44. *See*, 35 U.S.C. §154.

45. *See*, 35 U.S.C. §173; *see also* M.P.E.P §1505.

46. *See*, 35 U.S.C. §171 ("Whoever invents any new, original and ornamental design for an article of manufacture may obtain a patent therefor, subject to the conditions and requirements of this title.").

47. *See*, 35 U.S.C. §102; 35 U.S.C. §103.

48. *See*, 35 U.S.C. §154.

49. *See generally*, 37 C.F.R. §1.71 ("The specification must include a written description of the invention or discovery and of the manner and process of making and using the same, and is required to be in such full, clear, concise, and exact terms as to enable any person skilled in the art or science to which the invention or discovery appertains, or with which it is most nearly connected, to make and use the same.").

50. http://www.wipo.int/classifications/nice/en/preface.html (viewed on June 24, 2017).

51. https://www.uspto.gov/trademark/laws-regulations/office-policy-and-external-affairs-madrid-system-international (viewed on November 3, 2016).

52. International Patent Classification Version 2016, Guide to the IPC, World Intellectual Property Organization http://www.wipo.int/classifications/ipc/en/ (viewed on November 13, 2016).

53. http://www.wipo.int/classifications/ipc/en/ (viewed on December 29, 2016).

54. http://web2.wipo.int/classifications/ipc/ipcpub/#refresh=page&notion=scheme&version=20160101&symbol=D (viewed on November 13, 2016).

55. https://www.uspto.gov/learning-and-resources/general-faqs (viewed on November 3, 2016).

56. Ibid.

57. 2015 Special 301 Report, US Trade Representative, 2015, p. 6.

58. Ibid.

59. 2015 Special 301 Report, US Trade Representative, 2015, p. 51.

60. 15 U.S.C. §1127; *see also*, 19 CFR 133.21(a).

61. Section 526(e) of the Tariff Act of 1930 (19 U.S.C. §1526(e)), as implemented by 19 CFR §133.21.

62. https://iprr.cbp.gov (viewed on June 24, 2017).

63. 19 CFR §133.23.

Chapter 4

Marketing compliance for the fashion industry

Operating a successful fashion business in today's social and mobile marketplace requires a marketing campaign where targeted advertising occurs across a variety of mediums, be they traditional print or television advertisements, or more likely, a digital advertisement through which endless ways of connecting consumers to a brand exist. Given the breadth of options, it is critical to ensure that any marketing materials proposed for publication are not deceptive or otherwise misleading, as legal problems brought on by government allegations of wrongdoing can arise where instances of deceptiveness are found to exist.

Learning objectives

- Understand how to create non-deceptive advertising and marketing claims
- Determine what is required to use a celebrity endorsement and for how long it may be used
- Discern how to make clear and conspicuous digital disclosures
- Distinguish between an "unqualified" and "qualified" marketing claim

Who is regulating marketing claims?

The US Federal Trade Commission (FTC) governs the prevention of unfair or deceptive acts or practices, which includes print and online advertising, marketing, and sales messaging. Setting both the guidelines and parameters for determining when a marketing claim would be considered deceptive, the FTC also has enforcement powers to penalize those marketers and advertisers whose content it concludes is deceptive to the average consumer.

What kind of fashion marketing is at issue?

Fashion marketing comes in a range of forms, some of which are more readily recognizable than others. There are the traditional photo spreads seen in magazines, newspapers, and store catalogs with product information, and virtually all of these publications have brought this content online with some companies opting to eliminate their print versions altogether. Similar to a physical catalog, online stores likewise market their merchandise stating product features, fiber content, and all the other Required Information about wearing apparel which must be disclosed as set forth in Chapter 2. These statements, when used for marketing purposes, remain regulated by the FTC in terms of both mandatory disclosures and advertising.

An advertisement can come in all lengths and forms. It can range from a few words written on the face of a product's packaging or a hang tag on a garment, to that of a short digital advert in the form of a Reddit statement, or a 140 character "tweet" posted on Twitter®. There is also a form known as a **native advertisement**, which is where a product's marketing is incorporated into what appears to be a news article, or is such the case where a paid influencer promotes a product to its fan base of followers as if they were promoting it without being paid to do so.[1] While these ads may not necessarily look or appear to be an ad, when published by a company to promote its brand, they too are subject to compliance with the FTC's regulations as the Lord & Taylor native advertising case study at the end of this chapter exemplifies. More on native advertising is discussed later in this chapter.

The role of journalists and bloggers as influencers

For better or worse, with the ability of any consumer to broadcast its own opinion about a product or brand, companies are finding that customer opinion is ever increasingly shaping business decisions, putting "business as usual" under a microscope. Whereas fashion companies once had nearly exclusive control over their marketing messages via paid advertising, today fashion marketing is being shaped by journalists and bloggers who bring an ever greater spotlight on brands "doing good" or "bad," causing leading companies to rethink business practices due to the risks associated with unfavorable media exposure. Given the extent to which technology is being used as a lens into the reality of manufacturing and other "truths" in the fashion industry, I requested Jasmin Malik-Chua, Managing Editor of *E-Couterre.com*, an online guide to eco-fashion and sustainable style, to provide her perspective on the role of bloggers as influencers (Box 4.1). Her comments highlight the internet's ability to shape a conversation around a particular subject, in this case sustainability and the fashion industry, and how the immediacy of sharing digital content enables anyone to essentially become an influencer.

Box 4.1 Q&A: Jasmin Malik-Chua, Managing Editor of E-Couterre.com on bloggers as influencers

Jasmin and I first met when we shared the stage on a panel at NYC's Fashion Institute of Technology (FIT) at its 2012 Sustainable Fashion Conference. More than five years later, her blog—turned online fashion and lifestyle magazine—is ever growing and she lends us her insight on bloggers as influencers.

1. How would you assess the role of bloggers in making an impact on consumer thinking and decision-making in spending choices?

Bloggers, Instagrammers, and Youtubers, particularly those who focus on fashion and beauty, are the new influencers of the millennial age. I think it's because many of the looks they put together are more attainable than, say, those of a Hollywood celebrity.

2. Describe how you have seen the conversation around sustainable fashion grow and/or evolve as a result of blogging and other social media efforts.

Blogging and social media very quickly amplify the signal, almost in real time. There's an immediacy and intimacy that traditional media doesn't afford. The viral affect from instant sharing cannot be overemphasized, either, particularly in recent years, where almost everyone is plugged into some extent.

3. Do you think today a shopper is more conscientious about the clothes they are buying thanks to the efforts of authors and bloggers like yourself?

I certainly hope so! I think a major impediment to switching to a more sustainable lifestyle is information: what to buy, where to buy it, and so on. Blogs and websites can help break down the noise and service those needs by providing the relevant resources in fresh new ways, whether it's articles, slideshows, or videos. There are innumerable ways to harness modern technology to engage people, certainly more so than we had five, ten years ago.

Avoiding marketing problems with FTC

The FTC has some key baselines which can be followed to create truthful statements and avoid accidental configurations of information which could be considered deceptive. They include the "net impression standard," the making of a "qualified" or "unqualified" claim, and guidelines around the way in which a marketing claim may be crafted to be "clear and conspicuous," including the font size used and the placement and proximity of any qualifying language which may be added to an advertising statement. These precepts run with all forms of advertising and for this reason, this chapter begins with an examination of these general parameters.

FTC policy on deceptive advertising

The FTC takes a broad approach to the manner in which an advertisement may be considered deceptive. As has been the case for decades, it considers any representation, omission, or practice in advertising that would likely affect a consumer's conduct or decision making, with regard to a product or service, to be deceptive when it is likely to mislead consumers acting reasonably under the circumstances and is material.

Deceptive ads can come in many forms, including where a promotional message is not identifiable as advertising. The FTC believes that when consumers know the source of an advertisement, this typically affects the weight or credibility that consumers give it and that such knowledge may also influence whether and to what extent consumers choose to interact with the content in which the message is contained.[2] Therefore, deception is found to occur where the message misleads consumers into thinking it is an impartial or independent message when it is in fact, one from an actual advertiser.[3]

"Unqualified" vs. "qualified" marketing claims

Regardless of the type of marketing claim, there is one precept that underlies all of them which is that a claim may be "unqualified," or "qualified." An **unqualified marketing claim** is where only a blanket statement is made about a product, such as "Made in USA". A **qualified marketing claim**, on the other hand, is where there is a caveat that accompanies a blanket statement made about a product in order to specify to what extent such statement is truthful, such as

"Made in USA of Imported Fabric." As explained below, a qualified or an unqualified statement may be made whether it is with respect to an environmental, Made in America, or any other kind of marketing claim.

Incorporating qualifying information into an advertisement

Due to the requirement to use non-deceptive ads, a marketing statement should be evaluated in advance of publication to ensure it is likely to be clear and conspicuous. Considerations for making such an assessment, be it in hardcopy or a digital ad, include:[4]

- The location of a disclosure and its proximity to the relevant claim.
- The clarity of the disclosure as understood by the intended audience.
- Whether there is a need for repetition of a disclosure across a website.
- The extent to which other ad elements distract attention away from any disclosure.
- Whether visual disclosures appear for a sufficient duration.
- Where it is an audio disclosure, whether it is broadcast in an adequate volume and cadence.

When it is practical to do so, qualifying information should be incorporated into an advertisement to ensure such claim is clear and conspicuous, rather than having a separate disclosure to qualify a statement.

The "net impression" standard[5]

The FTC has a couple of different standards against which it measures how a consumer might interpret an ad. One such method is to assess the **net impression**, which evaluates whether an ad's overall format would be misleading rather than looking at the text in isolation.[6] Not only are the words used in the ad itself examined, this analysis also takes into account any visual or aural imagery, the interaction among all of the ad's elements, and what overall, or "net" impression, is left in the mind of the reasonable consumer.

Assessing the net impression of an online ad

Online advertisements, due in part to the breadth of creative elements available for making it, offer a wider range of possibilities for marketing a product. Due to the variations for creating an ad, some parameters to follow when evaluating whether or not an online ad may appear to be deceptive, include:

- The overall appearance;
- Dissimilarity of its written, spoken, or visual style to non-advertising content offered on a publisher's site; and
- The degree to which it is distinguishable from other content.[7]

Under what the FTC refers to as the *reasonable ad standard*, a marketer should ask itself when designing an ad, "How would a reasonable consumer interpret this?" Since interpretations that advertisers intend to convey about an advertisement's nature or source are presumed to be reasonable, any determination with respect to its deceptive nature will depend on how a reasonable consumer would interpret it in a particular situation.[8] This is especially true when a specific audience is being targeted in the ad, and therefore care must be taken to ensure only non-deceptive ads are published.

When deception occurs—categories of deceptive ads[9]

They are two primary ways in which the FTC has identified when and how deception can occur. The first is where an advertisement misleads consumers as to its true nature or source, including that a party other than the sponsoring advertiser is the source of a marketing message. Where this misrepresentation is **material**, meaning where it is likely to affect consumers' choices or conduct regarding the advertised product, then deception may be found to have occurred.

The second is where consumers are led to give greater credence to an ad's claim or to interact with advertising in which they otherwise would not have interacted, for example with a telemarketer or email ad. Misleadingly formatted advertisements may be considered deceptive even if the product or service claims communicated are truthful and non-misleading. The FTCs position is that when the first contact between a seller and buyer occurs through a deceptive practice, otherwise known as a **misleading door opener**, a law may be violated even if the truth is subsequently made known to the purchaser.[10]

Material facts

All findings by the FTC of a deceptive claim includes the presence of **material facts,** which are those facts that are important to consumer's choices or conduct regarding a product.[11] The FTC views any misrepresentation to be material when such advertising content, without qualifying that it is in fact an ad, is formatted as a news article, an independent product review, investigative report, feature article, or as scientific research. It further presumes that express claims and those an advertiser intended to make are material.[12] Therefore false claims that advertising and promotional messages reflect the independent and impartial views, opinions, or experiences of ordinary consumers or experts are also presumed material, and should be avoided.[13]

Guidance on digital advertising[14]

Whether by celebrity or organizational endorsements, targeted marketing, or native advertising, recent FTC cases show that there is no limit in the way deceptive advertising can be presented and that online advertising, even in a character limited environment such as on Twitter®, must nonetheless comply with the law. FTC drafting guidelines for making digital disclosures clear and conspicuous, include:

- Placing a disclosure as close as possible to the triggering claim.
- Reviewing the entire ad to assess whether the disclosure is effective in light of other elements—text, graphics, hyperlinks, or sound—that might distract consumers' attention from the disclosure.
- Accounting for the type of device or platform a consumer may use.

A complete list of the FTCs drafting guidelines may be found on the FTCs website at www.ftc.gov. It should be noted that where, even despite an advertiser's best effort to follow these parameters, a disclosure cannot be made clearly and conspicuously, then the ad should not be disseminated.[15]

Endorsements and testimonials in advertising[16]

The FTC defines an **endorsement** as any advertising message for which consumers are likely to believe is reflective of the opinion, finding, experience, or belief of the **endorser**, which could be an organization, a consumer, an expert, or a celebrity.[17] Endorsements can come in various forms, including demonstrations, depictions of personal characteristics of an individual, or their likeness, their name or signature, or verbal statements made by an endorser.[18]

To be considered a legally valid endorsement, an endorser must have been an actual user of the product at the time it was given and it must reflect their honest experience, opinions, beliefs, or findings.[19] Care should be taken so that the endorsement is not reworded or presented out of context, resulting in a distortion of the endorser's opinion or experience with the product.

Celebrity endorsements

Where the endorser is an expert or a celebrity, an ad may only continue to be run so long as the endorser is still using the product and continues to subscribe to the same views as originally presented in the ad.[20] In order to ensure this, an advertiser should secure the endorser's continued view of its endorsement either within reasonable intervals, or whenever there is a material alteration in the product, variations with its performance, or changes to a competitor's product where such a comparison is made.[21]

Expert endorsements[22]

The FTC defines an **expert** as an "individual, group, or institution possessing, as a result of experience, study, or training, knowledge of a particular subject, which knowledge is superior to what ordinary individuals generally acquire."[23] Where an ad purports that the endorser is an expert, they must have the qualifications to substantiate their possession of the expertise in relation to the endorsement message.[24] Their expertise must also be supported by an actual experience in evaluating the product's features or characteristics, and that such evaluated features are available to the ordinary consumer.[25]

Consumer endorsements[26]

Any ad that relays the experience of an endorser on the effectiveness, performance, or any other central point of a product will likely be viewed by a consumer as the endorser's personal experience. For this reason, an advertiser must have adequate substantiation for making consumer-endorsed claims, including competent and reliable evidence to support a claim about a product.[27] Where actual consumers are used in an ad, they must be used in both the audio and video portions of it. Where actors portraying real consumers are instead used, a statement that they are not actual consumers of the advertised product must be clearly and conspicuously disclosed.[28]

Native advertising[29]

Increasingly in digital media, ads are formatted in such a way that it is hard to distinguish where the words are in fact advertising due to the format matching, design style, and behavior of the digital media in which it is disseminated. This is known as native advertising and can be found in many digital formats, including social media posts, a news or news aggregator site, within a newsfeed, or through other means, including e-mail. They can also appear when embedded into either professionally produced or user-generated videos on social media, or other entertainment programming. Often these ads are inserted into the stream of regular content a publisher offers, appearing in the form of a short description, headline text, or thumbnail image, which if clicked, leads to additional content.

Due to the ease with which an ad can be deceptive when published in a digital environment, advertisers must take care to avoid an allegation by the FTC of deceptive marketing by a native ad. In evaluating an advertisement and whether a reasonable consumer would be able to distinguish it as a marketing message, the FTC will consider the particular circumstances in which the ad was disseminated, including the impression communicated by the ad's format, and the customary expectations based on a consumer's prior experience with the media in which it appears. Since the FTC requires that the advertising nature of the content is clear and conspicuous, a statement as to the published material being an ad itself should be asserted within a native ad.

How the targeted audience responds

The FTC looks not only at how a majority of consumers would have interpreted an ad but where, in fact, a significant minority of reasonable consumers are found to have been misled, it will be considered deceptive.[30] Since the propensity of natively formatted advertising to be misleading is greater due to its tailored messaging intended to appeal to the known preferences of a target audience, the FTC will consider the effect of an ad's format on ordinary and reasonable members of that specific group, and not the general public as a whole, as is the case with a country of origin claim on a product as explained below.

Making permissible country of origin and "Made in USA" claims

Whether it is made of wool, textile fibers, or fur, clothing and accessories made of any of these must have their country of origin disclosed on the product, and when a claim of it being Made in the USA is sought, it must comport to the guidelines set out in the FTC's Made in USA policy. Limitations on the permissible use of this statement date back over seventy years when the FTC established the principle that it was deceptive to market a product with an unqualified Made in USA claim unless it was wholly of domestic origin.[31]

The "all or virtually all" standard

To make an unqualified Made in USA claim, an advertised product must be **"all or virtually all" made in the US,** which means that all significant parts and processing that go into the product must be of US origin and contain either none, or merely a negligible amount of, foreign content.[32] To substantiate a claim of US origin under the "all or virtually all" standard, three factors to consider are:

1 The portion of any foreign materials to the total manufacturing costs;

2 Whether the principal assembly or final processing occurred in the US; and

3 How far removed from the finished product any foreign content is.[33]

Based on this evaluation, a marketer would be in a position to assert an unqualified "Made in USA" claim, or recognize that a qualified one should be used, for example, "Made in USA of Imported Fabric."

"Qualified" versus "unqualified" US origin claims[34]

A qualified Made in USA claim indicates the amount, extent, or type of a product's domestic processing or content and indicates that the product is not entirely of US domestic origin. An unqualified US origin claim like, "Made in America," indicates that with the possible inclusion of inconsequential amounts of material, a product is of US origin. It is imperative to evaluate if an origin claim may seem deceptive where it is not qualified. For example, if a company advertises its new textile product which was invented in California and manufactured in Vietnam as "Created in USA," FTC would consider this claim deceptive because of the likely interpretation of the term "created" correlating strongly in people's minds that the product was made in the USA. Therefore, as a general proposition, where the net impression could convey a deceptive message, a qualifying statement should be included.

FTCs country of origin rule on fashion merchandise

When stating the country of origin in advertising, mail order catalogs, or mail order promotional materials, there must be an indication that the product was imported, made in the USA, or both, and such statement must be consistent with the origin labeling of the product itself that is being advertised.[35] For fur, wool, or textile fiber products, the statement "Made in USA" or another equivalent term must be used if the product is completely made in the USA. Where partially made, the foreign origin together with a statement describing the partially manufactured portion of the product in the US must be disclosed, for example, "Hand carved in US – Silver from Peru."[36] Reference to other country of origin labeling requirements are discussed in Chapter 2 and Chapter 6.

"Green," "eco-friendly," and other sustainable fashion marketing claims

Sustainability is a leading topic of interest in today's fashion industry, both in terms of companies thinking about how to implement sustainable practices, and with respect to online magazines like "Ecouterre.com," that showcase environmentally friendly products and raise awareness of the toxicity and environmental damage caused by current apparel manufacturing processes.

In tandem with the rise of sustainable fashion, there has been a re-emphasis by the US government regarding the marketing of products that are claimed to be "eco-friendly" or "green." In fact, since the FTC's revamping of its *Guides for the Use of Environmental Marketing Claims* ("Green Guides") in 2013, there have been numerous cases brought by the FTC to prosecute companies accused of using deceptive marketing tactics, including the "bamboo" case study discussed in Chapter 2. While the Green Guides are not in fact the law, that is, the guides do not confer any rights on any person nor operate to bind the FTC or the public,[37] they are a series of guidelines intended to help marketers avoid making environmental claims that are unfair and deceptive under Section 5 of the FTC Act.[38] These are therefore important to follow, because where a claim is found to be misleading, the FTC can commence an enforcement action that results in significant monetary or other civil penalties.[39]

The purpose, scope and structure of the Green Guides[40]

As it relates to fashion, the Green Guides apply to claims made directly on labels, in advertising, or any other form of marketing and in any medium, including where implied by symbols, depictions, or logos, or directly stated in a product brand name or any other means.[41] They also apply to business-to-business transactions and to claims about the environmental attributes of a product, package, or service when made in connection with the marketing, offering for sale, or sale of such item or service to individuals.[42]

Distinctions between the benefits a product, package, or service confers[43]

Sometimes it is the packaging that contains the environmental benefit and other times the product or service itself being offered does. Whatever the case may be, the claim must specify to which part it is referring, and where it is applicable only to the product, package, or merely a portion of either of them, it must so specify. While there are exceptions, generally speaking, if the environmental attribute applies to all but minor incidental components of a product or package, the marketer need not qualify the claim to identify that fact.

Environmental marketing claims touted in the fashion industry[44]

"Eco-friendly" is one of the most visible environmental claims found in the marketing of fashion merchandise, which can convey that the product has far-reaching environmental benefits and give the impression that the product has little to no environmental impact. Some guidelines for minimizing deception when making environmental claims are illustrated in Box 4.2.

Box 4.2 Guidelines for minimizing deception when advertising as "eco-friendly"

Example: "Eco-Friendly – Made with Recycled Materials"

- Ensure the qualifying language, in this case "Made with Recycled Materials," is prominently displayed and clear.

- Ensure the ability to substantiate that with the exception of minor and incidental components, the entire product or package is made from recycled materials.

- Ensure the product is more environmentally beneficial overall having been made with recycled products.

- Ensure the ad's context does not otherwise imply other deceptive claims.

Recycled content claims[45]

It is commonplace to see statements about recycled content in the context of a paper or plastic bag, and now increasingly we are seeing it in relation to fashion merchandise. Under the FTCs guidelines, **recycled content** includes used, reconditioned and re-manufactured components, as well as recycled raw materials.[46] Though it is popular to indicate that an article is "good" for the environment, unless it is 100 percent made of recycled content, excluding minor incidental components, it is deceptive to make an unqualified statement that it contains recycled materials.

Where it is partially made with recycled material, in order to not be considered deceptive, qualifying this claim by indicating the amount or percentage by weight of recycled content in a finished package or product is required.[47] With regards to goods composed of materials that have been recovered or otherwise diverted from the waste stream, either during the manufacturing process (pre-consumer) or after consumer use (post-consumer),[48] either distinguishing between these two or indicating the percentage of pre-consumer or post-consumer content may be stated to avoid making a misrepresentation. Box 4.3 provides an example of such a case.

Box 4.3 Acceptable waste stream recycling example

A manufacturer collects excess fabric from the original clothing manufacturing process. After minimal reprocessing, it combines these fabric scraps with virgin material for use in the same product. A recycled content claim would not be considered deceptive since the fabric waste would normally have entered the waste stream and would not normally have been reused by the industry.

Unless it is obvious that a product's recycled content consists of used, reconditioned, or re-manufactured components as exemplified in Box 4.4, a product should clearly and prominently qualify the recycled content claim to avoid deception about the nature of such components.[49]

Box 4.4 Unacceptable recycling example

A store sells both new and used clothing and accessories. One of the items for sale in the store is a Fedora hat, which although used, is no different in appearance than a brand new item. The hat bears an unqualified "recycled" label. This claim is deceptive because reasonable consumers would likely believe that the hat is made of recycled raw materials, when it is in fact, a used item. An acceptable claim would bear a disclosure clearly and prominently stating that the hat was "used" and not recycled.

Environmental certifications and seals of approval[50]

An environmental certification or seal of approval likely conveys that the product offers a general environmental benefit and, for this reason, a company marketing such a designation should ensure a specific or limited benefit is referred to in order to avoid deception. Endorsements, logos, or a seal of approval by an independent third party is also considered deceptive where there is no qualifying language, and so care should be taken that any endorsement meets the FTCs criteria. In addition, a company must have substantiation for all claims reasonably communicated through the endorsement, logo, seal, or certification.

Guidelines for online representations of overseas shipping[51]

Sellers of merchandise sold online, by mail, or over the phone must be in a position to have their sold goods shipped within the timeframe stated on their website, or within thirty days where no delivery designations are provided.[52] A failure to do this will be considered a deceptive practice by the FTC. For this same reason, seller's must provide the buyer with revised timeframes where the original shipping dates cannot be met, and where it is known that merchandise will not be shipped after all, a seller must either offer to the consumer an ability to consent to a delay in the shipping, or to receive a full refund.[53]

Violations and penalties for non-compliance

Deceptive marketing violations fall into the same penalty structure as that of findings of misbranding, discussed in Chapter 2, as they both result in violations of Section 5 of the FTC Act.[54] Reference should be made to that chapter for further information on potential penalties.

Considerations for your own marketing compliance

To help companies follow FTC mandates, the agency has several online publications, guides, and other notices which can all be found on its website at www.ftc. gov and, at the time of publication, were at the links cited below. These should be referenced when crafting a marketing campaign in order to minimize any potentially deceptive acts. Due to the variations in potential forms of marketing claims together with the FTC's subjective nature of their determinations of wrongdoing however, it should be noted that while the application of the FTC's guidance may not always be cut and dry, its mandate that all marketing be non-deceptive is. Therefore, the resources listed below should be considered whenever advertising or promotional messages are being created and upon finalization, discussions with your attorney to verify legalities should likewise be considered.

FTC electronic resources for more information

- *Advertising FAQ's: A Guide for Small Business:*[55] https://www.ftc.gov/tips-advice/business-center/guidance/advertising-faqs-guide-small-business
- *Dot.com Disclosures:*[56] https://www.ftc.gov/sites/default/files/attachments/press-releases/ftc-staff-revises-online-advertising-disclosure-guidelines/130 312dotcomdisclosures.pdf
- *Enforcement Policy Statement on Deceptively Formatted Advertisements:*[57] https://www.ftc.gov/system/files/documents/public_statements/896923/151 222deceptiveenforcement.pdf
- *Guides Concerning Use of Endorsements and Testimonials in Advertising:*[58] https://www.ftc.gov/sites/default/files/documents/one-stops/advertisement-endorsements/091005revisedendorsementguides.pdf
- *Guides for the Use of Environmental Marketing Claims:*[59] https://www.ftc.gov/enforcement/rules/rulemaking-regulatory-reform-proceedings/green-guides
- *Native Advertising: A Guide for Business:*[60] https://www.ftc.gov/tips-advice/business-center/guidance/native-advertising-guide-businesses

Key terms

"all or virtually all" made in the US endorsement endorser expert	material material facts misleading door opener native advertising net impression	qualified marketing claim recycled content unqualified marketing claim

Discussion questions and exercises

1 Explain the difference between a "qualified" and an "unqualified" claim.

2 If cotton fabric manufactured in the US is sent to Mexico and made into pajamas, how would a non-deceptive origin advertisement be written?

3 For how long may an advertiser continue to use a celebrity endorsement?

4 Name at least three factors a marketer should take into consideration when drafting a clear and conspicuous digital disclosure for use on a website viewed on multiple types of devices, e.g., laptop, smart phone, etc.?

Case study FTC claims retailer Lord & Taylor violated FTC's marketing rules

Lord & Taylor's 2015 dress campaign that involved paying fashion influencers to promote merchandise via social media without any disclosures as to the paid nature of the influencer's endorsements was found to be misleading and hence, considered a violation, by the FTC of its endorsement regulations.

This campaign involved the use of Instagram® images and captions reflecting the statements of seemingly impartial fashion influencers who were actually paid endorsers. It generated 328,000 brand engagements and reached 11.4 million individual users. Not only did the failure to disclose these influencer's endorsement status result in allegations of multiple violations, but the deceptive advertising was exacerbated by the company's false representation in an article published in online fashion magazine, *Nylon*, about the dress which appeared to reflect an independent opinion when it was really a paid ad.

The result? FTC found these acts to be a deceptive use of native advertising which resulted in three separate violations being issued due to the lack of any disclosure as to the paid nature of the marketing. It should be noted that whenever a connection exists between an endorser and a seller of an advertised product which is not readily apparent, and therefore, is likely not going to be known by the audience, and which might materially affect the weight or credibility of the endorsement, such connection must be disclosed.[61]

FTC's advice? When considering a native advertising campaign, disclose any and all material connections between your company and the advertisers, endorsers, and influencers that might materially affect the weight or credibility a consumer would give to the endorsement or advertising, in order to stay within FTC's marketing parameters and keep your business out of trouble.[62]

Notes

1. https://www.ftc.gov/tips-advice/business-center/guidance/native-advertising-guide-businesses (viewed on June 24, 2017).
2. https://www.ftc.gov/system/files/documents/public_statements/896923/151222 deceptiveenforcement.pdf (viewed on June 24, 2017).
3. Ibid.
4. *Dot.com Disclosures – How to Make Effective Disclosures in Digital Advertising*, p. i, March 2013.
5. FTC Enforcement Policy Statement, p. 11; 16 CFR §260.2(d).
6. *FTC v. Am. Home Prods. Corp.*, 695 F.2d 681, 687 (3d Cir. 1982), citing *Beneficial Corp. v. FTC*, 542 F.2d 611, 617 (3d Cir. 1976).
7. https://www.ftc.gov/system/files/documents/public_statements/896923/151222 deceptiveenforcement.pdf (viewed on June 24, 2017).
8. FTC Enforcement Policy Statement, p. 11.
9. FTC Enforcement Policy Statement, p. 7, 10, 14–15.
10. Deception Policy Statement, 103 F.T.C. at 180 & n. 37.
11. *Kraft, Inc. v. FTC*, 970 F.2d 311, 322 (7th Cir. 1992).
12. Deception Policy Statement, 103 F.T.C. at 182.

13. FTC Enforcement Policy Statement, p. 15.
14. *Dot.com Disclosures – How to Make Effective Disclosures in Digital Advertising*, p. i, March 2013.
15. *Dot.com Disclosures – How to Make Effective Disclosures in Digital Advertising*, p. iii, March 2013.
16. 16 CFR §255.1; 16 CFR §255.0(b).
17. 16 CFR §255.0(b).
18. Ibid.
19. 16 CFR §255.1(a)–(c).
20. 16 CFR §255.1(c).
21. 16 CFR §255.1(b).
22. 16 CFR §255.13; 16 CFR §255.0(e).
23. 16 CFR §255.0(e).
24. 16 CFR §255.3(a).
25. 16 CFR §255.3(b).
26. 16 CFR §255.2(a).
27. *See generally*, 16 CFR §255.2.
28. 16 CFR §255.2(c).
29. FTC Enforcement Policy Statement, p. 10 and 11.
30. FTC Statement on Deception, 103 F.T.C. 174, 177 (1984) (appended to *Cliffdale Assocs., Inc.*, 103 F.T.C. 110 (1984)) ("Deception Policy Statement").
31. *See, Windsor Pen Corp.*, 64 F.T.C. 454 (1964); *Vulcan Lamp Works, Inc.*, 32 F.T.C. 7 (1940).
32. https://www.ftc.gov/tips-advice/business-center/guidance/complying-made-usa-standard (viewed on June 26, 2016).
33. 62 FR 63756, 63765 (1997).
34. FTC's *Complying with the Made in USA Standard*, p. 7, December, 1998; 16 CFR 303.33, 62 FR 637769.
35. 16 CFR §300.25a, 16 CFR §303.34.
36. *See*, 16 CFR §301.16, 16 CFR §301.17, 16 CFR §300.25, and 16 CFR §303.33.
37. 16 CFR §260.1(a).
38. 15 USC §45.
39. 16 CFR §260.1(b).
40. 16 CFR §260.1(a)–(d).
41. 16 CFR §260.1(c).
42. Ibid.
43. 16 CFR §260.3(b).
44. 16 CFR §260.4(d).
45. 16 CFR §260.13.
46. 16 CFR §260.13(a).

47. 16 CFR §260.13(c).

48. 16 CFR §260.13(b).

49. 16 CFR §260.13(d).

50. 16 CFR §260.6.

51. 16 CFR §435.2.

52. 16 CFR §435.2(a).

53. 16 CFR §435.2(b)(i).

54. 15 USC §45.

55. https://www.ftc.gov/tips-advice/business-center/guidance/advertising-faqs-guide-small-business (viewed on July 6, 2016).

56. https://www.ftc.gov/sites/default/files/attachments/press-releases/ftc-staff-revises-online-advertising-disclosure-guidelines/130312dotcomdisclosures.pdf (viewed on July 6, 2016).

57. https://www.ftc.gov/system/files/documents/public_statements/896923/151222 deceptiveenforcement.pdf (viewed on July 6, 2016).

58. https://www.ftc.gov/sites/default/files/documents/one-stops/advertisement-endorsements/091005revisedendorsementguides.pdf (viewed on July 6, 2016).

59. https://www.ftc.gov/enforcement/rules/rulemaking-regulatory-reform-proceedings/green-guides (viewed on July 6, 2016).

60. https://www.ftc.gov/tips-advice/business-center/guidance/native-advertising-guide-businesses (viewed on July 6, 2016).

61. 16 CFR §255.5.

62. https://www.ftc.gov/news-events/press-releases/2016/03/lord-taylor-settles-ftc-charges-it-deceived-consumers-through (viewed on October 1, 2017).

Chapter 5

Flammability testing and issues specific to children's products

The flammability testing of clothing for adults and children's sleepwear are two of the most frequently performed lab tests done on wearing apparel and represent one of the best known hazards in the fashion industry—flammable fabrics.

Learning objectives

- Identify which types of fabrics are exempt from flammability testing
- Understand what a certificate of compliance is and when it is required
- Distinguish the ways in which a product's compliance may be guaranteed
- Understand the myriad of rules that apply to children's products

The law as a means to prevent flammable wearing apparel dates back to 1953 when the Flammable Fabrics Act (FFA) was enacted. This law, together with its rules and regulations, provides the framework within which this prevention effort continues today and is commonly referred to as the Flammability Standard.[1] Its purpose is twofold. The first is to prevent individuals from wearing clothing and fabrics so highly flammable as to be dangerous, and the second is to prohibit the sales, marketing, handling, or shipping of such merchandise.

Wearing apparel is generally recognized under the Flammability Standard as any costume or article of clothing worn or intended to be worn by individuals, with the exception of hats, gloves, and footwear.[2] When it is intended or sold for use in wearing apparel, the term **fabric** means any material that is woven, knitted, felted, or otherwise produced from, or in combination with, any natural or synthetic fiber, film, or substitute thereof.[3] Interlining fabrics however, such as those found in a suit, would not be considered a fabric where they are (1) intended or sold for use in wearing apparel, and are (2) intended for incorporation into an article of wearing apparel as a layer between an outer shell and an inner lining.[4]

The Flammability Standard and its purpose

The Flammability Standard establishes three classes of flammability and sets forth the standards and methods for testing the flammability of clothing and fabrics.[5] Its requirements apply to all fabrics or related materials that are in a form or state ready for use in an article of wearing apparel.[6]

Flammability and surface textile fabrics

As is well known, everything at a certain temperature is capable of catching on fire. Flammability in the context of this standard does not therefore imply that a fabric will never catch on fire but rather that it will not do so at a particular ignition rate. **Flammability** means those characteristics of a material that pertain to its relative ease of ignition and relative ability to sustain combustion.[7] The three flammability classes under this standard distinguish flammability levels based on whether the fabric is a plain surface textile, or a raised surface textile. A **plain surface textile fabric** is any textile fabric which does not have an intentionally raised fiber or yarn surface such as a pile, nap, or tuft, but does include those fabrics that have fancy woven, knitted or flock-printed surfaces.[8] A **raised surface textile fabric**, such as velvet or other pile fabrics on the other hand, has an intentionally raised fiber or yarn surface.[9]

The three classes of flammability

A fabric's class of flammability is determined by an actual test of the fabric. Class 1 textiles are those which exhibit normal flammability, Class 2 textiles an intermediate flammability, and Class 3 textiles a rapid and intense burning.[10] Fabrics in Classes 1 and 2 are acceptable for use in clothing, whereas those in Class 3 must not be used for clothing as they are considered dangerously flammable due to their rapid and intense burning.

Flammability testing

When used for clothing, some fabrics are potentially dangerous to the wearer because of the speed and intensity of the flame with which they burn, their ease of ignition, and because of the garment's design. The first two of these factors can be measured, and those measurements together with a visual observation of the flame's intensity permits the separation of different fabrics into three classes of flammability, thus enabling a decision as to a fabric's suitability for clothing.[11]

Basic test methodology

Only uncovered or exposed parts of wearing apparel need to be tested for purposes of determining its flammability, as the Flammability Standard considers a garment too dangerous to be worn where its uncovered or exposed parts exhibit rapid and intense burning when tested.[12] An **uncovered or exposed part** means that part of an article of wearing apparel that might be susceptible to a flame or other means of ignition when worn under normal use, as well as linings with exposed areas.[13]

Certified test lab parameters

There are some basic parameters every certified test lab must follow when testing a fabric. First, the test must be conducted on a fabric that is in a state or form ready for use in wearing apparel.[14] Second, a preliminary trial must be conducted to determine either the quickest burning direction or, in the case of a raised surface textile, the most flammable surface.[15] Lastly, there are specific guidelines for mounting, brushing and conditioning the test specimens, the exam procedure itself, and a requirement to test a textile before and after refurbishing, i.e., dry cleaning and laundering.[16] For these and other reasons, testing must be performed by a US government certified test lab, as discussed later in this chapter.

Exemptions from flammability testing

Not all fabrics require flammability testing. This is because from years of testing under the Flammability Standard, despite being able to catch fire at a certain temperature, for purposes of clothing, these fabrics are considered non-flammable.

Exempted fabrics

Fabrics recognized as being non-flammable are

- acrylic, polyester, wool, modacrylic, nylon, olefin, or
- plain surface fabrics weighing 2.6 ounces per square yard or more, irrespective of their fiber content.[17]

Where fabrics are in a form or state ready for use in wearing apparel, and are made of one or more combinations of these fibers, they too are exempt from any test requirement to support a guaranty of its non-flammability.[18]

Exempt products

When products, including wearing apparel and costumes, are made entirely from one or more of the exempted fabrics listed above, they too are exempt from any requirement for testing to support guaranties of those garments.[19] In addition, subject to certain exceptions, veils, hats, gloves, handkerchiefs, footwear, and interlining fabrics are exempt from the Flammability Standard, and therefore are not subject to testing for flammability, as they are not considered wearing apparel.[20]

Guaranties that wearing apparel and fabrics are non-flammable

The US Consumer Product Safety Commission (CPSC) has enforcement authority over the regulations governing flammable fabrics. Due to the importance placed by the CPSC on the non-flammability of clothing, it requires that sellers provide a guarantee (spelled "guaranty" in the regulations) as to a product's compliance with the law. A guarantee may be represented in either a "separate guaranty" or a "continuing guaranty," as further explained below. Generally speaking, when a seller has received a guaranty in good faith, it may be relied upon as a bar to prosecution where an allegation of wrongdoing has arisen. This means that if, for example, children's pajamas were found to be flammable and the CPSC brought a penalty action against the retailer selling them, a showing of a guaranty of non-flammability related specifically to these pajamas would indicate its reasonable reliance on the manufacturer's representation as to their non-flammability, and could prevent prosecution of that retailer by the CPSC. For this reason, it is recommended that a retailer request a guaranty from the importer, manufacturer, or distributor at the time of purchase. By doing so, it can operate confidently knowing that it is selling lawful products in addition to having this record readily available for recordkeeping purposes in the event an allegation is raised by the CPSC.

Initial guaranties of non-flammability

To demonstrate a product's compliance with the Flammability Standard, an initial guaranty may be issued by a seller who either, (1) received a guaranty from the party it purchased the merchandise from, or (2) hired a test lab to perform reasonable and representative tests on their products in order to support its initial guarantee of them. The term **program of reasonable and representative tests** means at least one test which is the subject of an initial guaranty, with results demonstrating conformance with the Flammability Standard performed either within or outside of the territories of the US.[21] As long as the test lab is one that is certified by the CPSC, it can be located in another country and there are several based outside of the US. For an initial guaranty, a program of reasonable and representative tests may consist of one or more tests of the particular fabric, class of fabrics, or related materials.[22] The term **class** in this sense refers to a category of fabrics or related materials having general constructional or finished characteristics, and which are covered by a description generally recognized in the trade.[23]

A separate guaranty of non-flammability

Wearing apparel may undergo multiple production runs of the same product or merely a singe run. When it is the latter, a seller may issue an individual guaranty which is known as a **separate guaranty**. It is valid where the date, signature and address of the **guarantor**, i.e., the person certifying the guaranty, is provided and the guaranty is based upon:

- Tests performed by or for the guarantor;
- A guaranty received in good faith from another party that had testing performed; or
- Where permitted, the testing of a class of goods was done.[24]

Language regarding a guaranty may be incorporated into an invoice or it can be presented in its own document. When it is the latter, there are two ways a guaranty may be done which is either as a general statement of compliance, or an indication that it is based on another's guaranty.[25]

The use of a continuing guaranty and its filing requirement

Rather than preparing a separate guaranty for every shipment, a **continuing guaranty** may be filed with the CPSC that is applicable to any product, fabric, or related material that is marketed or handled by the guarantor.[26] It is good for an initial three years, and must be renewed every three years thereafter or at any such time as there is a change in the legal business status of the company filing the guaranty.[27]

Requirement to reside in the US

An important requirement to note is that in order to file a continuing guaranty, the person or company that is the guarantor must reside in the US.[28] This is particularly relevant as the ability for someone to rely upon a guaranty as a bar to prosecution will cease to exist where the guaranty was received from someone who is not a resident of the US.[29] For this reason, among others, any time there is a change to the address of the principal office, place of business, or legal status of the filer of a guarantor, the CPSC must be notified immediately.[30]

Requirement for a certificate of compliance

A domestic manufacturer or an importer must certify its product's compliance with all rules and regulations under the Consumer Product Safety Act (CPSA), which includes compliance under the Flammability Standard.[31] Such certification, known as a **general certificate of conformity** (GCC), is either based upon the reasonable and representative testing of merchandise for which the results were satisfactory, or upon reliance on another person's certificate of compliance. An example of this would be where a shirt manufacturer relies on the GCC of its fabric supplier as to its non-flammability.

In the case of foreign made goods, a GCC indicates their compliance with all applicable CPSA laws,[32] and it must be available for CPSC inspection upon the shipment's arrival to the US.[33] In the case of a product manufactured in the US, only the manufacturer must be in a position to certify that the goods comply with all applicable CPSA laws prior to their introduction into domestic commerce, e.g., their sale to a retailer.[34]

Content and form of certificate

While it may also be in other languages, certificates of compliance must be in English and can exist in hard copy or electronic form.[35] The content should contain all such data listed in Box 5.1 and though not required, it is recommended to be contained in a single page. Certificates of compliance must

---

Box 5.1 Contents of certificate of compliance[37]

1 Identification of the product covered by the certificate.

2 Citation to each CPSC product safety regulation or statutory requirement to which the product is being certified identifying separately each applicable consumer product safety rule or regulation that is applicable to the product.

3 Name, full mailing address, and telephone number of the importer or domestic manufacturer certifying compliance of the product.

4 Contact information for the individual maintaining records of test results, including the custodian of records' name, e-mail address, full mailing address, and telephone number.

5 Date and place (including city and state, country, or administrative region) where the product was manufactured.

6 Date and place where the product was tested for compliance.

7 Identification of any third-party laboratory upon whose testing the certificate depends, including the name, full mailing address, and telephone number of the laboratory.

---

accompany each product or shipment and be furnished to each distributor and retailer of the product in question with a means to verify the date of its creation or last modification.[36] This should be kept in mind when the material in Chapter 6 on imports is analyzed, as the GCC and its availability with a shipment takes on an additional dimension of accountability with respect to foreign-made products and importer oversight.

The recordkeeping requirement under the flammability rules

Under the FFA, records must be kept for a period of three years. Those ordinarily required to furnish guaranties, along with those who are manufacturers of articles normally exempt from the Flammability Standard but who are nonetheless makers of hats, gloves, footwear, or interlining fabrics from flammable fabrics, are also required to keep records which show the (1) acquisition, (2) end use, and (3) disposition of such fabrics.[38] It is important to note that anyone who furnishes a guaranty but neglects or refuses to maintain and preserve records in a compliant manner will be considered to have furnished a false guaranty.

Recordkeeping requirement of importers of flammable fabrics or apparel

An importer of flammable fabrics or apparel must maintain records that establish the imported fabrics or articles of wearing apparel had been shipped for appropriate flammability treatment, and that such treatment had been completed.[39] It must also retain any records regarding the disposition of the shipment subsequent to the completion of such treatment.[40]

Enforcing the flammability laws

When any fabric or article of wearing apparel is so highly flammable as to be dangerous, the following activities are considered prohibited transactions:[41]

1 their manufacture for sale, the offering for sale, or actual sale in commerce;

2 their importation into the United States;

3 their introduction, delivery for introduction, transportation, or for the purpose of sale or, delivery after their sale, in commerce.

It is also prohibited to market or handle such goods when, after having been properly tested, they are nonetheless still found to be so highly flammable as to be dangerous when worn by individuals.[42]

Penalties

Penalties can be levied by the CPSC against any retailer, manufacturer, importer, distributor, or any other legally responsible party who knowingly violates the FFA.[43] A civil penalty can be as high as $100,000 for each violation, unless a death occurred in which case it can be as high at $250,000 for an individual and $500,000 for an organization.[44] For any series of violations, the maximum civil penalty can go as high as $15,000,000.[45] The CPSC will analyze the **statutory factors**, i.e., those it is mandated to follow for making a penalty determination, such as the occurrence or absence of an injury and its severity. The CPSC can also consider the totality of the circumstances and all other facts concerning a violation, including the size of a business, its ability to pay a penalty, and any aggravating factors.[46] Imprisonment for a maximum of five years for a knowing and willful violation, together with a fine, may also be imposed.[47] For these reasons as well as, more importantly, for the safeguarding of human life, compliance with the Flammability Standard is of paramount importance and should be taken very seriously.

The concern over children's product safety

Risks involving the flammability of children's clothing is just one of the many hazards recognized with children's products. When it comes to products for children, safety cannot be overemphasized as there are many hazards present for children by virtue of their growth, developmental stages and behaviors.

Who is regulating issues related to children's apparel?

Like the Flammability Standard, the CPSC has oversight of compliance with several other rules that apply to children's products. An increase in enforcement activity and oversight was seen following the 2008 Consumer Product Safety Improvement Act (CPSIA) which ushered in a variety of new certification and testing requirements that retailers, manufacturers, importers, and distributors are now responsible for complying with. Specifically, preventing injuries to children by **substantial product hazards**, which are product defects that create a substantial risk of injury for reasons such as the severity of the risk or the pattern of defect, were of particular concern.[48]

Identifying requirements on children's products

When it comes to children's products, and in particular wearing apparel, the primary compliance issues include:

- maximum lead limits in products;
- maximum lead levels in surface coatings and paints;
- the tracking label;
- small parts; and
- flammability issues.

How to determine when you have a children's product

Children's products are those designed or intended primarily for children twelve years of age or younger.[49] There are four key legal factors that must be considered as a whole to determine when a product is indeed a "children's product":[50]

1 A statement by a manufacturer about the intended use of a product.

2 Representations in its packaging, display, promotion, or advertising that it is appropriate for use by children twelve years of age or younger.

3 A common recognition by consumers that it is intended for use by a child twelve years of age or younger.

4 The CPSC Age Determination Guidelines which indicate that a product is one used by children.

Express and implied representations

Representations indicating that a product may or may not be one for children can be express or implied.[51] For example, advertising by a manufacturer expressly declaring that the product is intended for children twelve years of age or younger will support a determination it is a children's product, while an image of children twelve years of age or younger using the product implies that the product is one for children. These representations may be found in the packaging, words, illustrations or photographs depicting consumers using the product, instructions, assembly manuals, or advertising media used to market the product.[52] Other factors which distinguish children's products from non-children's products include colors, costs, safety features, decorative motifs correlated to childhood (e.g., insects or animals), and exaggerated features such as large buttons.[53]

Children's sleepwear and flammability issues

The CPSC has two special flammability regulations dedicated to children's sleepwear. One is known as the "Standard for the Flammability of Children's Sleepwear: Sizes 0 through 6X (FF 3–71)," and the other as the "Standard for the Flammability of Children's Sleepwear: Sizes 7 through 14 (FF 5–74)."[54] Under these rules there are specific tests which must be done and the passing result can be used as the basis for claiming compliance with either of these standards.

Children's sleepwear and infant garments

Children's sleepwear is any product of wearing apparel, either up to and including size 6X, or sized 7 through 14, including nightgowns, pajamas, or similar and related items, such as robes, which are intended to be worn primarily for sleeping or activities related to sleeping, except diapers and underwear, infant garments, and tight-fitting garments.[55] An **infant garment** is that which is sized for nine months or younger, or is a one-piece garment which does not exceed 64.8 centimeters (25.75 inches) in length, or if a two-piece garment, has no piece exceeding 40 centimeters (15.75 inches) in length.[56] Certifying compliance with the CPSC's non-flammability of children's sleepwear rules must be based upon the regulations set forth under these two standards.

Hazards recognized with children's products

To evidence that a product is not a danger to children, it must be certified based upon testing conducted by a CPSC accepted test lab, which technically is referred to as a **third party conformity assessment body**.[57] Of primary concern is that of children's lead poisoning due to its harmful impact on the renal, hematopoietic, and nervous systems, for which exposure can lead to seizure disorders, blindness, behavior disorders, and death.[58]

Lead paint and other surface coatings

Whether it is a t-shirt with a silk-screened image on it or some other article intended to be entrusted to, or for use by children, where some paint or other surface coating is placed on to a children's product that contains lead-containing paint, it is considered a banned hazardous substance. **Lead-containing paint** is any paint or other similar surface coating material containing lead or lead compounds where the lead content exceeds 0.009 percent by weight of the total nonvolatile content of the paint, or the weight of the dried paint film.[59] Paint and other similar surface-coating materials are a fluid, semi-fluid, or other material which changes to a solid film when a thin layer is applied to a metal, paper, leather, cloth, plastic, or other surface.[60] Care must be taken to ensure that lead-based paints and surface coatings are not on children's clothes or other articles intended for children.

Lead content

While no longer recognized as an issue with fabric dyes, lead content may nonetheless be found in objects sewn in, or otherwise connected to clothing, such as in a zipper or snap. The CPSC's acceptable lead limit in products is capped at 100 ppm (parts per million) unless the CPSC determines that the lower limit is not technologically feasible.[61] A functional purpose exception from this stringent minimum may be granted where three specific requirements are met:[62]

1 The inclusion of lead is required because it is not otherwise practicable or technologically feasible to manufacture.

2 Under normal use and abuse patterns, it is not likely to be placed in the mouth or ingested.

3 There are no measureable adverse effects on public health or safety.[63]

Lead and fabric

In 2015, the CPSC determined that dyes which are organic chemicals that can be dissolved and made soluble in water or another carrier so that they penetrate into a fiber, and textiles made from these dyes, do not contain lead.[64] The effect of this decision resulted in the lifting of the prior requirement to subject such products to a test lab and certification.[65] Importantly, dyed textiles are not subject to required testing for lead in paint or for total lead content, regardless of the techniques used to produce such materials and apply such colorants, so long as those materials have not been treated or adulterated with materials that could add lead, and are one of the following natural or manufactured fibers:[66]

- Natural fibers (dyed or undyed): Cotton, kapok, flax, linen, jute, ramie, hemp, kenaf, bamboo, coir, sisal, silk, wool (sheep), alpaca, llama, goat (mohair, cashmere), rabbit (angora), camel, horse, yak, vicuna, qiviut, guanaco.

- Manufactured fibers (dyed or undyed): Rayon, azlon, lyocell, acetate, triacetate, rubber, polyester, olefin, nylon, acrylic, modacrylic, aramid, spandex.

It is important to note that just because this is applicable to dyes that could be applied to textiles at the fiber, yarn, fabric, or finished product stage, textiles which have paints and pigments that are directly applied on to the textile product, or added to the surface of the textiles, like decals, transfers, and screen printing, could indeed contain lead, and are therefore subject to the testing required under the CPSIA for children's products.[67]

Children's metal jewelry and lead concerns

When it comes to metal jewelry, a child's exposure to lead is the hazard at issue. Jewelry may be considered as intended or designed for children twelve years of age or younger based upon its size, theme, and the way it is marketed to children. Characteristics indicative of jewelry being considered a children's product include the size, low cost, childish themes on the jewelry, play value, or its packaging graphics and text.

Inaccessible component parts

Lead limits do not apply to component parts of a product that are not accessible to a child, i.e., those not physically exposed by reason of a sealed covering or casing, and those which do not become physically exposed through reasonably foreseeable use and abuse of a product, including swallowing, mouthing, breaking, or other children's activities, nor the aging of the product.[68]

The small parts rule

The CPSC regulates articles intended for use by children under three years of age which present a choking, aspiration, or ingestion hazard because of its small parts.[69] While the application of this rule would apply to many products other than children's clothing, it is important to note that where sequence or other decorative articles are considered for placement on children's apparel, and particularly so for those under three years old, they will likely present a choking hazard and should be reconsidered if not eliminated.

Other children's hazards—drawstrings

One of the most commonly found hazards on children's apparel is a **drawstring**, which is a non-retractable cord, ribbon, or tape of any material that pulls together parts of upper outerwear to provide for closure.[70] ASTM F 1816–97 is a safety specification for drawstrings on children's upper outerwear in sizes 2T to 16 or the equivalent, and where the garment has one or more drawstrings it must be in conformance with this specification.[71] Where this type of outerwear has one or more drawstrings that are not in conformance with this specification, it is considered a *substantial product hazard* by the CPSC.[72]

Requirement to test and certify children's products

As explained earlier in this chapter, a certificate of compliance is the document which a manufacturer or importer uses to represent that the product it is selling conforms to all applicable CPSC laws. Manufacturers and importers of children's products are required to select representative product samples and submit a sufficient number of them to a CPSC approved test lab for testing.[73] Where the products pass the lab test, a children's product certificate (CPC) may be issued that is based upon such initial test or periodic testing.[74]

Periodic testing plan and testing interval

Manufacturers and importers must develop a periodic testing plan to ensure with a high degree of assurance that children's products manufactured after the issuance of a CPC, or since the previous periodic testing was conducted, continue to comply with all applicable children's product safety rules. A periodic testing plan, specific to each children's product manufactured at a particular site, must be in place which includes the tests to be conducted, the intervals at which the tests will be conducted (which cannot exceed one year), and the number of samples tested.[75] Where a material change in the product's design, manufacturing process, or component parts sourcing occurs, then the testing of this modified product should be undertaken for the issuance of a new CPC as such change could have affected the product's ability to comply with the applicable regulations.[76]

Reliance on component part testing

Component part testing can be used whenever tests on a component part will provide the same information about the compliance of the finished product as would be provided by tests of the component after it is incorporated into or applied to a finished product.[77] A **component part** is any part of a consumer product, including a children's product, that either must, or may, be tested separately from a finished consumer product in order to assess its ability to comply with a specific regulation enforced by the CPSC.[78] Component part testing may only be relied on to support a CPC where the testing procured is **traceable**, meaning where all testing parties are identifiable, including their name and address, which could be a manufacturer, supplier, or test lab.[79] The component part testing rule is intended to give all parties involved in testing and certifying the flexibility to procure or rely on required certification testing where such testing is easiest to conduct or the least expensive.[80] The only limitation to this is that where the law requires the testing of the entire finished product, a manufacturer or importer certifying compliance may not rely on component part testing in these instances.[81]

How to find a test company

To find a lab, the CPSC website at www.cpsc.gov has a page entitled "List of CPSC-Accredited Testing Laboratories" through which the location or type of test may be input as a search parameter and certified test labs are identified for use.

Mandatory tracking label rule

US manufacturers and importers are subject to compliance with the **children's tracking label** rule, which requires information be placed on a children's product to enable its source and other production information.[82] It must be visible, legible, and permanently placed on products that are designed or intended primarily for use by children aged twelve and younger, and contain the manufacturer or private labeler's name, the location and date of the product's manufacture, and information about the manufacturing process.[83]

Recordkeeping for children's apparel and products

A manufacturer or importer of a children's product subject to a CPSC safety rule is subject to the maintenance of several records which must be kept for five years. They include, but are not limited to:

1 A copy of the CPC for each product.

2 Records of each third party certification test for each manufacturing site.

3 Test records about a children's product, including a periodic test plan, periodic test results and component part test results, or the testing of representative product samples.

4 Records of descriptions of all material changes in product design, manufacturing processes, and sourcing of component parts.

Records must be made available for inspection by the CPSC upon request and may be maintained in languages other than English if they can be translated accurately into English and submitted within forty-eight hours of a request.[84]

Violations and penalties for non-compliance with children's rules

Violations can arise from the mere failure to maintain records adequately, to that of the product being non-compliant with a CPSC regulation. Other acts that can lead to a violation include, but are not limited to, a failure to have test certificates, certifying compliance from tests done at non-CPSC certified labs, and failing to exercise due diligence in relying on third-party certifications.[85] While the CPSC could require a company to periodically submit reports on its ongoing compliance practices, the CPSC could also issue monetary penalties which could be as high as $100,000 for each violation, and for any series of violations the maximum civil penalty can go as high as $15,000,000.[86]

Applicability of laws to small batch producers

A **small batch manufacturer** is one who has manufactured no more than 7,500 units of the same product and whose total gross revenues of all consumer products from the prior calendar year is $1,086,627 or less.[87] When designated as a "small batch manufacturer," the requirement to test products at a CPSC certified test lab in order to certify compliance to certain regulations is not required, however testing for children's product safety rules is always required.[88]

While initially this may sound like one less requirement that a small company would need to deal with, the reality is that most of the required testing remains obligatory on children's products, as this designation does not change the requirement to test under the lead paint limits, small parts rule, or children's metal jewelry rule.[89]

In conclusion, irrespective of the requirement to test or not test products, it is important to remember that the requirement that the products are *in fact* compliant remains. Initial and periodic testing are therefore still recommended as a regular business practice by small batch manufacturers, not only to safeguard the lives of those using their products, but also to safeguard their business from the inadvertent sale of non-compliant goods which could ultimately lead to penalties or other ramifications.

Key terms

children's products	guarantor	separate guaranty
children's sleepwear	infant garment	small batch
children's tracking label	interlining fabrics	manufacturer
class	lead-containing paint	statutory factors
component part	material change	substantial product
continuing guaranty	plain surface textile	hazards
crocking	fabric	third party conformity
drawstring	program of reasonable	assessment body
fabric	and representative	traceable
flammability	tests	uncovered or exposed
general certificate of	raised surface textile	part
conformity	fabric	wearing apparel

Discussion questions and exercises

1 You have an order of pajamas being manufactured in Istanbul, Turkey for children aged eight years old. You plan to import this merchandise into the US.

   (a) Under what standard of flammability is testing of the pajamas subject to?

   (b) The Children's Product Certificate must state the product's compliance to what CPSC standard in order to lawfully enter the US?

   (c) Research the CPSC website and provide the name, address, telephone number and website address (URL) of an Istanbul, Turkey based CPSC certified test lab you would use to perform the required exams.

2 As a seller of men's jackets, must you test the outer shell, interlining, and inner lining of the jacket for flammability? Or would it be permitted to only test some of these parts?

Case study CPSC product recalls in fashion [90]

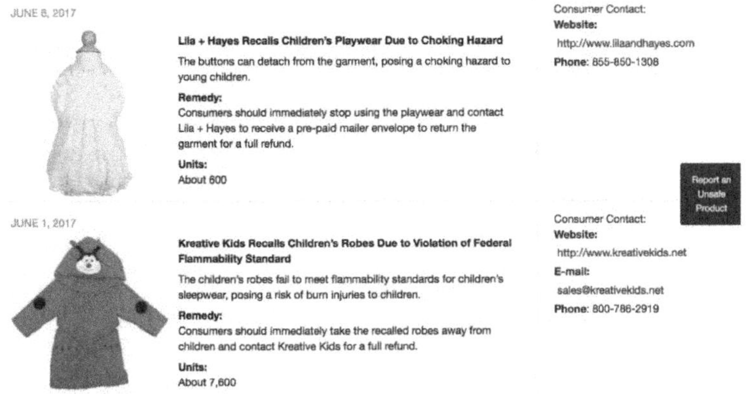

JUNE 8, 2017

Lila + Hayes Recalls Children's Playwear Due to Choking Hazard
The buttons can detach from the garment, posing a choking hazard to young children.

Remedy:
Consumers should immediately stop using the playwear and contact Lila + Hayes to receive a pre-paid mailer envelope to return the garment for a full refund.

Units:
About 600

Consumer Contact:
Website:
http://www.lilaandhayes.com
Phone: 855-850-1308

Report an Unsafe Product

JUNE 1, 2017

Kreative Kids Recalls Children's Robes Due to Violation of Federal Flammability Standard
The children's robes fail to meet flammability standards for children's sleepwear, posing a risk of burn injuries to children.

Remedy:
Consumers should immediately take the recalled robes away from children and contact Kreative Kids for a full refund.

Units:
About 7,600

Consumer Contact:
Website:
http://www.kreativekids.net
E-mail:
sales@kreativekids.net
Phone: 800-786-2919

Figure 5.1 CPSC product recall webpage listing of two apparel companies subject to a product recall. Source: United States Consumers Product Safety Division.

In less than one week, the CPSC issued two product recalls on children's wear. One in relation to a violation of the Flammability Standard on a robe, and the other in relation to a choking hazard posed by the buttons on a garment. As shown on the product recall webpage (https://www.cpsc.gov/Recalls) (Figure 5.1), instructions on how to return the article and obtain a refund are provided for consumers to follow. For the seller's part, not only must it facilitate the return and refund of each product (7,000 in the case of the robes), but it further has the burden of complying with ongoing CPSC reporting requirements, both of which are unavoidably costly and time consuming.

Box 5.2 Q&A: Interview with Adam Varley of CPSC Certified Lab, Vartest Labs

Adam Varley, Co-Founder of Vartest Laboratories, Inc. in New York City's famed Garment District lends his advice on working with a CPSC certified test lab.

What advice would you give for someone who is new to working with a test lab and needs to have fabric tested?

When a fabric sample is submitted, make sure your request is clear regarding what test(s) you need and how fast you need the results. Be sure to send enough fabric for the test(s) to be performed, in general one yard, full width, assuming its 60 inches in width which is the typical width of a yard.

Make sure your samples are clearly marked, preferably permanently written with indelible ink or on a label stapled to the fabric (or it could fall off), identifying on the face of the fabric its details, which can include the style, lot, color number, or some other reference. Occasionally I've seen the name of the test is written on the sample but that's not typically done. Also when sending a fabric sample, send it with the selvedge so the lab can figure out which end is up since the directionality may be important in testing.

How would your advice differ with wearing apparel?

It is usually best to submit the largest size you have and its best to send two samples so that the lab has one original to compare the tested one to, whether in relation to color or size, in the case of shrinking.

What are the typical types of tests clients want to have performed?

The most common test of apparel retailers is **crocking** [i.e., the tendency of dye to rub off of a fabric due to dyeing methods, penetration or post-dyeing treatments[91]] and shrinkage, then flammability and fiber content. There's also a lot of testing for traditional product performance specifications, which are comprised of:

Construction: Fabric weight, fabric, count, yarn size.

Physical testing: Seam slippage, tensile strength, tear strength for performance standards—generic standards and then specific ones made by public and private entities, e.g., prisons or the military, which can involve a two step process, first you test and then you decide if it passes or fails.

Colorfastness: Crocking, light fastness.

What's new in the world of garment testing?

We are seeing a lot of high tech fabrics that companies are making claims on now, and they want it tested for the presence of whatever property they are trying to claim regarding the fabric, such as wicking finishes or anti-bacterial finishes.

Contact information for Adam Varley: avarley@vartest.com, tel. (212) 947–8719.

Notes

1. *See*, Standard for the Flammability of Textiles (16 CFR Part 1610).
2. 15 USC §1191(d); 16 CFR Part 1610.
3. *See*,15 USC §1191(f).

4. 16 CFR §1610.1(c)(4).

5. 16 CFR §1610.1(b).

6. 16 CFR §1610.1(a).

7. 16 CFR §1610.2(e).

8. 16 CFR §1610.2(k).

9. 16 CFR §1610.2(l).

10. 16 CFR §1610.1(b).

11. 16 CFR §1610.2, Notes Applicable to Entire Subpart.

12. 16 CFR §1610.33(a); 16 CFR §1610.34.

13. 16 CFR §1610.31(g).

14. 16 CFR §1610.6(a).

15. 16 CFR §1610.6(a)(2) and (3).

16. 16 CFR §1610.2(m).

17. 16 CFR §1610.1(d).

18. 16 CFR §1610.1(e).

19. 16 CFR §1610.1(d).

20. 16 CFR §1610.1(c).

21. 16 CFR §1610.37(c)(2).

22. 16 CFR §1610.37(c)(1).

23. 16 CFR §1610.37(c)(3).

24. 16 CFR §1608.2.

25. Ibid.

26. 16 CFR §1608.3(a).

27. Ibid.

28. 16 CFR §1608.3(a).

29. 16 CFR §1608.4.

30. 16 CFR §1608.3(a).

31. 16 CFR §1110.1(a)(1).

32. 16 CFR §1110.7(a).

33. 16 CFR §1110.7(a) and (c)(1).

34. 16 CFR §1110.7(c)(2).

35. 16 CFR §1110.9.

36. 16 CFR §1110.13(a)–(b).

37. 16 CFR §1110.11.

38. 16 CFR §1610.36.

39. 16 CFR 1610.39(c)(1).

40. Ibid.

41. 16 CFR §1610.39.

42. 16 CFR §1610.32.

43. 16 CFR §1119.2; 16 CFR §1119.3(c).

44. 18 USC §3571.
45. 15 USC §1194(e)(1).
46. 16 CFR §1119.4.
47. 15 USC §1196.
48. 16 CFR §1120.2(a).
49. 16 CFR §1500.90(a).
50. 16 CFR §1200.2(a).
51. 16 CFR §1200.2(c)(2)(i).
52. 16 CFR §1200.2(c)(2).
53. 16 CFR §1200.2(c)(3).
54. 16 CFR §1615 and 16 CFR §1616, respectively.
55. 16 CFR §1615.1(a); 16 CFR §1616.2.
56. 16 CFR §1615.1(c).
57. 80 FR 61729, 61730 dated October 14, 2015.
58. 16 CFR §1303.5(a)(2).
59. 16 CFR §1303.2 (b)(2). The current level became effective August 14, 2009.
60. 16 CFR §1303.2 (b)(1).
61. 16 CFR §1500.89.
62. 78 FR 41298 dated July 10, 2013.
63. 78 FR 41298 dated July 10, 2013 (no measureable adverse effect will be considered to exist where no increase in blood lead levels of a child exist).
64. *See generally*, 80 FR 61729, 61731 dated October 14, 2015.
65. Ibid.
66. Ibid.
67. Ibid.
68. 16 CFR §1500.87(b).
69. 16 CFR §1500.18(a)(9).
70. 16 CFR §1120.2(c).
71. 16 CFR §1120.3.
72. Ibid.
73. 16 CFR §1107.21(f).
74. 16 CFR §1107.2.
75. 16 CFR §1107.21(b)(1).
76. 16 CFR §1107.2.
77. 80 FR 61729, 61730 dated October 14, 2015.
78. 16 CFR §1109.4(b).
79. 16 CFR §1109.4(m); 16 CFR §1109.5(f).
80. 80 FR 61729, 61730 dated October 14, 2015.
81. 16 CFR §1109.5(c).
82. 15 USC §2063(a)(5).

83. Ibid.

84. 16 CFR §1107.26.

85. 15 USC §2068.

86. 15 USC §2069. These figures are subject to an inflationary increase in 2017.

87. http://www.cpsc.gov/en/Business--Manufacturing/Small-Business-Resources1/ Small-Batch-Manufacturers-and-Third-Party-/ (viewed on May 28, 2016).

88. Ibid.

89. Ibid.

90. https://www.cpsc.gov/Recalls (viewed on July 7, 2017).

91. *See*, *Fairchild's Dictionary of Fashion*, 2nd Edition, Revised, Fairchild Publications, a division of ABC Media, Inc., p. 147, 1998.

Chapter 6

Importing fashion merchandise

In Chapter 1, it was mentioned that the legal framework governing the fashion enterprise turned on several factors, one of which was in relation to where the merchandise originated from. When a company opts to purchase and import goods made in another country, it is electing to comply with a distinct set of customs laws that imported products are subject to. Declarations, product markings, certifications, value determinations, and the complete submission of such data and a corresponding payment of customs duties to the government can get complicated fast. Since from the government's perspective importing is a privilege and not a right, the ability to participate in international trade hinges on one's capacity to comply with import laws and the procedures that accompany it. This chapter sets forth a general overview of the processes and procedures for the legal compliance of imported fashion merchandise.

Learning objectives

- Identify fashion compliance obligations in the context of importing
- Discover the many import declarations required on fashion imports
- Understand the key documentary framework to an importation
- Decipher how to read the US Harmonized Tariff Schedule

Importing 101—a global system

If you look around the average American household today you will quickly discover that most of the articles there are from other countries. You would find the same result when examining the labels on your wearing apparel and may even realize that 100 percent of your clothes have been imported with much of it from China, as the 2015 dollar value in apparel imports from China alone totaled $30,540,941,000.[1]

With so much wearing apparel being made on foreign shores, it follows that a complex legal system exists to regulate the import and export of fashion and other merchandise around the world. To streamline these transactions globally, organizations have been created to maintain a uniform set of trade rules across countries. Two such organizations are the World Customs Organization (WCO) and the World Trade Organization (WTO).

Who are the WCO and WTO?

Each country has a government agency responsible for regulating the lawful entry of foreign goods through their own domestic borders. Known generically as a **customs agency**, it governs how commercial goods are processed before, at the time of, and after importation, including which forms must be submitted and what data must be declared. It is also responsible for collecting **customs duties**, which is a product-specific tax assessed on imported merchandise and payable to the government at the time of importation.

World Customs Organization

Rather than having a world with dozens of different sets of customs rules, the World Customs Organization (WCO) promotes the security and facilitation of international trade through the simplification and harmonization of customs procedures and revenue collection.[2] Comprised of 180 members and representing more than 98 percent of global trade, the WCO is responsible for developing the **Harmonized System** (HS) which is the nomenclature for international goods that enables products to be identified by the same classification code all over the world.[3] Known in the US as the *Harmonized Tariff Schedule of the United States*, or simply the *HTSUS*, each imported product has a specific **tariff classification number**, which is the classification code that is recognized globally under the HS as this product.

World Trade Organization

The World Trade Organization (WTO) oversees trade facilitation, the global rules of trade between nations, and it ensures that trade flows as smoothly, predictably, and as freely as possible.[4] Today's WTO trade agreements provide the foundation for international commerce and ultimately, at least in theory if not always in practice, binds the governments of member countries to keep their trade policies open and non-discriminatory.[5] It is through the structure created by the WCO and WTO that the structure and protocols for today's importing environment exists, which is consistently applied across most countries globally.

The basic predicates to any importation

Within the global framework set forth by the WTO and WCO, each country has established its own import laws with the collection of customs duties as a primary goal due to these monies funding government activities. Importantly, collecting the appropriate amount per shipment is achieved by an importer's truthful and accurate declaration of (1) the value of the imported merchandise (2) its tariff classification number(s), and (3) the proper identification and marking of the product's country of origin. This data is submitted by an importer to the customs agency who analyzes and ultimately approves or denies the goods for entry into the county. The customs authority has several other additional responsibilities, including but not limited to, dealing with trade security, excluding goods that violate intellectual property laws, and in many countries, supervising exports.

US Customs and the HTSUS

American customs procedures and tariff laws are governed by the US Department of Homeland Security's (DHS) Bureau of Customs and Border Protection (US Customs or CBP). When it comes to how US Customs makes decisions about imports, it is required to do so against the rules and structure set forth in the HTSUS, which is maintained by the US International Trade Commission (USITC). The HTSUS is organized by sections which contain several chapters. Within each chapter are lists of product descriptions, classification numbers, duty rates, and other detailed information on thousands of goods. These descriptions must be followed when making a determination about a product's tariff number.

The structure of the HTSUS and the products categorized in each section and chapter of the tariff itself, go from basic materials to complex products. In the case of clothing for example, the section in which garments are classified, namely, HTSUS Section XI for "Textiles and Textile Articles" shown in Figure 6.1, starts with the basic fiber of "Cotton" in Chapter 50 and ends with not

Figure 6.1 Section XI of the HTSUS. Source: US International Trade Commission.

merely new goods, but already used ones under Chapter 63 entitled, "Other made up textile articles; sets; worn clothing and worn textile articles; rags."[6] Each of the chapters in Section XI relate to textiles or textile articles and it is here where fabric, clothes and other textile fiber and wool products (*see* Chapter 2) are largely classified.

The tariff classification and duty rate of imported merchandise

Goods are classified in order to determine the correct rate of duty, to levy an accurate amount of customs duties on an imported shipment, and to collect the data for tracking imports and import trends. The HTSUS' "General Rules of Interpretation" (GRI) (Figure 6.2) sets forth the guidelines on how imports must be classified.

The GRIs shown in Figure 6.2 are a hierarchical list for which the classification of imports specifically states that as an initial proposition (*see* GRI 1 in Figure 6.2) "classification shall be determined according to the terms of the headings and any relative section or chapter notes . . ." related to a specific product.[7] Where these are not sufficient for a determination, then and only then, would the subsequent principles set forth in the GRIs, namely GRIs 2 through 6, govern.[8]

How to read the tariff

Each product is assigned a ten-digit tariff classification number and every importer in its declaration to US Customs is responsible for making an accurate

Harmonized Tariff Schedule of the United States (2016) Supplement-1
Annotated for Statistical Reporting Purposes

GN p.1

GENERAL RULES OF INTERPRETATION

Classification of goods in the tariff schedule shall be governed by the following principles:

1. The table of contents, alphabetical index, and titles of sections, chapters and sub-chapters are provided for ease of reference only; for legal purposes, classification shall be determined according to the terms of the headings and any relative section or chapter notes and, provided such headings or notes do not otherwise require, according to the following provisions:

2. (a) Any reference in a heading to an article shall be taken to include a reference to that article incomplete or unfinished, provided that, as entered, the incomplete or unfinished article has the essential character of the complete or finished article. It shall also include a reference to that article complete or finished (or falling to be classified as complete or finished by virtue of this rule), entered unassembled or disassembled.

    (b) Any reference in a heading to a material or substance shall be taken to include a reference to mixtures or combinations of that material or substance with other materials or substances. Any reference to goods of a given material or substance shall be taken to include a reference to goods consisting wholly or partly of such material or substance. The classification of goods consisting of more than one material or substance shall be according to the principles of rule 3.

3. When, by application of rule 2(b) or for any other reason, goods are, prima facie, classifiable under two or more headings, classification shall be effected as follows:

    (a) The heading which provides the most specific description shall be preferred to headings providing a more general description. However, when two or more headings each refer to part only of the materials or substances contained in mixed or composite goods or to part only of the items in a set put up for retail sale, those headings are to be regarded as equally specific in relation to those goods, even if one of them gives a more complete or precise description of the goods.

    (b) Mixtures, composite goods consisting of different materials or made up of different components, and goods put up in sets for retail sale, which cannot be classified by reference to 3(a), shall be classified as if they consisted of the material or component which gives them their essential character, insofar as this criterion is applicable.

    (c) When goods cannot be classified by reference to 3(a) or 3(b), they shall be classified under the heading which occurs last in numerical order among those which equally merit consideration.

4. Goods which cannot be classified in accordance with the above rules shall be classified under the heading appropriate to the goods to which they are most akin.

5. In addition to the foregoing provisions, the following rules shall apply in respect of the goods referred to therein:

    (a) Camera cases, musical instrument cases, gun cases, drawing instrument cases, necklace cases and similar containers, specially shaped or fitted to contain a specific article or set of articles, suitable for long-term use and entered with the articles for which they are intended, shall be classified with such articles when of a kind normally sold therewith. This rule does not, however, apply to containers which give the whole its essential character;

    (b) Subject to the provisions of rule 5(a) above, packing materials and packing containers entered with the goods therein shall be classified with the goods if they are of a kind normally used for packing such goods. However, this provision is not binding when such packing materials or packing containers are clearly suitable for repetitive use.

6. For legal purposes, the classification of goods in the subheadings of a heading shall be determined according to the terms of those subheadings and any related subheading notes and, mutatis mutandis, to the above rules, on the understanding that only subheadings at the same level are comparable. For the purposes of this rule, the relative section, chapter and subchapter notes also apply, unless the context otherwise requires.

Figure 6.2 HTSUS general rules of interpretation. Source: US International Trade Commission.

determination about a product based upon the description provided in the tariff. As shown in Figure 6.3, the HTSUS under the "Rates of Duty" part of the table (on the right-hand side) contains three different columns which are representative of the trade relationship the US has with a country or regional trading partner.

Those with whom the US has normal trade relations will receive the duty rate in Column 1 (General), whereas those with whom the US has a preferential or free trade agreement with, as designated in Column 1 (Special), receive a reduced rate of duty. Those countries with whom the US has no particular

Harmonized Tariff Schedule of the United States (2016) Supplement-1
Annotated for Statistical Reporting Purposes

XI
61-4

Heading/ Subheading	Stat. Suf- fix	Article Description	Unit of Quantity	Rates of Duty		
				General	Special	2
6101		Men's or boys' overcoats, carcoats, capes, cloaks, anoraks (including ski-jackets), windbreakers and similar articles, knitted or crocheted, other than those of heading 6103:				
6101.20.00		Of cotton..	....	15.9%	Free (AU, BH, CA, CL, CO, IL, JO, KR, MA, MX, OM, P, PA, PE, SG)	50%
	10	Men's (334)...	doz. kg			
	20	Boys' (334)...	doz. kg			
6101.30		Of man-made fibers:				
6101.30.10	00	Containing 25 percent or more by weight of leather (634)...	doz. kg	5.6%	Free (AU, BH, CA, CL, CO, IL, JO, KR, MA, MX, OM, P, PA, PE, SG)	35%
		Other:				
6101.30.15	00	Containing 23 percent or more by weight of wool or fine animal hair (434)............................	doz. kg	38.6¢/kg + 10%	Free (AU, BH, CA, CL, CO, IL, JO, KR, MA, MX, OM, P, PA, PE, SG)	77.2¢/kg + 54.5%
6101.30.20		Other..	....	28.2%	Free (AU, BH, CA, CL, CO, IL, JO, KR, MA, MX, OM, P, PA, PE, SG)	72%
	10	Men's (634)...	doz. kg			
	20	Boys' (634)...	doz.			

Figure 6.3 HTSUS heading 6101. Source: US International Trade Commission.

trade relationship with are subject to the duty rate shown in Column 2, for which a significantly higher rate of duty is assessed.[9] It should be noted that these countries are treated differently from those with whom the US has trade embargoes against or otherwise does not have normal trade relations with, such as Syria. With these countries the US simply does not engage in any trade with them.

How to classify a product—boy's jacket example

The first eight out of ten digits in a tariff classification number are in the "Heading/Subheading" column (Figure 6.3) with the last two numbers located in the "Statistical Suffix" column next to it. Using the HTSUS image as a reference (Figure 6.3), a boy's ski jacket made of cotton has a classification number of 6101.20.0020 and is subject to a 15.9 percent general rate of duty when imported from countries the US has normal trade relations with. The jacket has a free, i.e., 0 percent rate of duty when it originates from any of the countries with whom the US shares a trade agreement as denoted in the "Special" column identified by a single or two-letter code. An example of this is the code "BH," which stands for the United States-Bahrain Free Trade Agreement Implementation Act and indicates that goods with this tariff number originating from Bahrain qualify for a tariff assessment of 0 percent.

The country of origin and marking requirement

Generally speaking, every article of foreign origin or its container is required to be marked under the Customs laws with its country of origin so that the **ultimate purchaser**, that is, the last person in the US who will receive the article in the form in which it was imported, can readily know where it came from.[10] In the US, each product must be legibly marked with the English name of the country in a conspicuous place and as indelibly and permanently as the nature of the article, or its container, will permit.[11]

The marking requirement is applicable to all imported goods into the US and is a distinct law separate from that of the FTCs country of origin requirement on wearing apparel (*see* Chapter 2). Where fashion merchandise is being imported, it should be noted that both FTC and CBP laws must be abided by.

Specific country of origin rules on apparel and textile products

Generally speaking, under the customs regulations a **textile or apparel product** is any good classifiable in Chapters 50 through 63 of the HTSUS.[12] US Customs has specific guidelines on how to determine the **country of origin of an apparel or textile product**, and defines the term as the "country, territory, or insular possession in which a good originates, or of which a good is the growth, product, or manufacture."[13] US Customs has numerous other instructions on how to make origin determinations when involving, for example, knit to shape and finished garments, fabrics, and products that are **wholly assembled**, i.e., where at least two components pre-existed in essentially the same condition as found in the finished good yet were combined to form the finished good in a single country, territory, or insular possession.[14]

Customs rules when the use of words suggest an import is of US origin

US Customs is concerned about any words, letters, or names that may mislead or deceive the ultimate purchaser as to a product's actual country of origin. In order to prevent this, it has specific regulations to address cases in which the words "USA," "American," the "United States," or any other variation of such words or letters are combined with another country that is the actual country of origin on a product.[15] The same regulations also address the case where a US city or locality is identified on an import, or where a product mentions a foreign country or locality which differs from where the article was actually manufactured or produced.[16] Where this occurs, there must also be in close proximity to such words, names, or letters, the actual country of origin together with the words "Made in," "Product of," or other words of similar meaning preceding it.[17] These words must be permanently and indelibly placed in at least a comparable size of the actual name of the country of origin and appear on the same side or surface of the product.[18]

When the name of a place other than the country of origin appears in a trademark

There are times where the name of a place other than the country of origin may appear as part of a trademark or trade name. US Customs has a specific regulation to address this which requires (1) the actual country of origin to appear in either a conspicuous location or within close proximity to such place or name and (2) be preceded by text "Made in," "Product of," or words of similar meaning.[19] An example of this is shown in Figure 6.4, where the Henri Bendel New York brand is labeled on an imported product, and the words "New York" are in a font smaller than that of the words "Made in China," yet in close proximity to such country of origin.

Figure 6.4 Country of origin is labeled in close proximity to the trademark name. Source: Deanna Clark-Esposito.

Substantial transformation

As described above, Customs has specific regulatory guidelines regarding origin determinations on apparel and textiles. It also has a general definition of the **country of origin** that covers all goods and is defined as the country of manufacture, production, or growth of any article of foreign origin entering the US.[20] More specifically, it is generally based upon the country in which the last major manufacturing step took place that resulted in the article taking on its final form. It is from this general definition that the concept of "substantial transformation" derives and it is commonly applied to wearing apparel as components for a product, such as a woman's brassiere, are shipped from various countries to another for manufacturing where labor costs are lower. A **substantial transformation** occurs when an article emerges from a process with a new name, character, or use which is different from that possessed by the article prior to the processing, and will not merely result from a minor manufacturing or combining process that leaves the identity of the article intact.[21] The result is that the product obtains the country of origin designation of such country where this last process took place.

Determining the correct country of origin is essential, not only because of the potential for delays and penalties which could ensue as a result of an incorrect designation, but also because in many articles, such as watches, some of the markings are on the inside of the article and therefore have to be addressed in advance of manufacturing. Post-manufacturing corrections are difficult and expensive and should be avoided at all costs.

Value

An accurate assessment of the value of imported merchandise is critical to make as it is upon this amount that customs duties are calculated and assessed. Determining the value for customs purposes however, is not always as clear-cut as one might think. This is because Customs calculates the value of goods based upon anything that contributed to the import value of a product and not merely the costs indicated by the seller on its invoice. Rather, Customs would include other inputs contributing to its dutiable value, for example the cost of any components that the importer sent to the factory for inclusion in the imported product. While customs laws provide multiple methods upon which the value can be determined, the most common is to value imports on the basis of its "transaction value."

Transaction value

Transaction value is the "price actually paid or payable" for merchandise when sold for exportation to the US, plus the amounts for other items if not included in the seller's price.[22] Such items include packing and packaging, tooling, designs, labels, materials, selling commissions, and any proceeds from a subsequent sale shared with the factory.[23] Where these amounts are not included in the seller's price, for example where the importer bears the costs for the hangers upon which it wants their garments shipped, then they too become part of the dutiable value. The duty assessment is therefore based on the seller's invoice plus the costs incurred for the hangers. There are times where materials, tooling, certain designs, or other things which are absolutely necessary to be able to make the product or to sell it to the US, will be provided or paid for by an importer independent of the invoice price of the goods. These items, which are effectively provided to the factory free of charge or for less than their fair market value, should be added to the transaction value or invoice price when declaring values to Customs.

The term **price actually paid or payable** means the total payment (whether direct or indirect, and exclusive of any costs, charges, or expenses incurred for transportation, insurance, and related services incident to the international shipment of the merchandise from the country of exportation to the place of importation in the US) made, or to be made, for imported merchandise by the buyer to, or for the benefit of, the seller.[24] Such sales price is that negotiated at an arm's length between unrelated sellers and buyers where the seller knows that the goods are being sold for shipment to the US. If, for reasons due to the complexity of the transaction itself, the transaction value cannot be used to determine the dutiable value, then an alternative valuation method may be used, such as by determining the value of identical or similar merchandise, or another method.

Getting your goods "cleared" through customs

In order for imported goods to obtain customs clearance or "clear customs," as is commonly stated in the trade, and be granted admission into the US, an import declaration must be filed with US Customs in the form of a customs entry. It may be filed by the **importer of record**, i.e., the owner or purchaser of the cargo, or as is more typically done, by their licensed **customs broker**, which is a party licensed by US Customs who files the entry documents on behalf of the importer of record pursuant to a fully executed power of attorney. Importers must also obtain a **bond**, which is a monetary pledge to abide by US Customs laws, including making a correct classification and value determination, as well as paying the duties owed. Customs brokers often assist an importer with obtaining this as well.

The importer of record is obliged to use reasonable care in making entry and in all dealings it has that relate to US Customs.[25] As CBP analyzes the data provided on the entry form and accompanying shipping documents to determine whether a shipment may be admitted into the US, this not only means ensuring that the data provided on the entry form is accurate but also that notifications to other federal agencies, as appropriate, have been made and where required, that product testing to meet the regulatory requirements by such agencies have been done so that every law governing a product is complied with at the time of importation. An example of this would be the General Certificate of Conformity (GCC) discussed in Chapter 5.

Making a "formal" entry

It is not uncommon to hear the term "entry" used as both a noun and a verb, which can describe the act of getting merchandise cleared through US Customs (verb) as well as the paper work involved in doing so (noun). Even Customs own regulations defines the term entry in this way:

Noun—the documentation or data required to be filed with the appropriate
    CBP officer or submitted electronically to the Automated Commercial
    Environment (ACE) or any other CBP-authorized electronic data
    interchange system to secure the release of imported merchandise from
    CBP custody.
Verb—the act of filing that documentation.[26]

Making what is known as a "formal entry" is required where a shipment's value is greater than $2,500 and it entails the filing of certain obligatory records and forms which ultimately enables the cargo's release from CBP custody.

The entry filing

The **entry filing** includes the deposit of estimated duties and any accompanying entry summary documentation or data required for CBP to assess duties, collect statistics, and determine a shipment's legality in relation to other laws which is a precondition to the release of imported merchandise from CBP custody.[27] Where goods are valued at less than $2,500, a less arduous process known as an "informal entry" may instead be made, at least under most circumstances, and can often be done by an individual without the need to engage a customs broker.[28]

Liquidation

Just because a shipment cleared US Customs and has been received by the importer does not mean that the agency approved the admissibility of the merchandise. A final confirmation of admissibility occurs upon **liquidation**, which is the final computation of duties on an entry, and oddly enough, can take place several months after the cargo has been received by an importer, and even distributed thereafter to the ultimate purchaser.[29] Even though CBP has made this final determination does not mean the importer is necessarily happy with it for reasons such as a difference of opinion about the country of origin or tariff classification and hence, the duty rate paid (or owed) which could be higher than originally anticipated by an importer. Where it is believed that CBP erred in its final determination, however, a challenge may be brought against its decision by filing a petition known as a **protest** within 180 days of the merchandise being liquidated. This mechanism must be utilized for an importer to contest a decision made by US Customs, whether or not regarding a product's classification, if seeking an adjustment or refund of duties and for various other reasons.[30] This results in a re-examination of the shipment's data itself, together with other information an importer may provide. While no outcome is guaranteed, this formal petition and review process is available for an importer to take advantage of.

Imports and fashion merchandise

All imports must comport to US Customs laws at the time of importation. Regarding fashion imports, this means that all required activities and documents, whether it is product testing, labeling products with their fiber content and care instructions, the preparation and filing of other declarations, or certifying compliance with the FTC's rules, must be done in advance of the shipment's arrival to the US or risk being delayed, or denied entry, at the border.

What is fashion compliance for importers?

In the context of importing, fashion compliance obligations can be identified by those activities that occur (1) prior to the good's leaving the foreign factory and (2) those that occur in advance of their arrival to the US, as set forth in Box 6.1. Several of these acts done to fashion merchandise need to be declared to the CBP.

Common fashion-related import declarations on fashion merchandise

Import declarations on fashion merchandise extend beyond the customs entry and the required invoice details. Following the Consumer Product Safety Improvement Act of 2008 (CPSIA),[31] the requirement to have a general certificate of conformity "accompany" a shipment became obligatory, and as has been the case for several decades, where a product contains elements of certain animal species, then the requirement to complete a US Fish and Wildlife Department (USFW) certificate may also be triggered.

The General Certificate of Conformity

As explained in Chapter 5, when it comes to fashion merchandise, the Consumer Product Safety Commission (CPSC) requires a General Certificate of Conformity (GCC) to accompany a shipment certifying an importer's compliance with FTC laws, which in the case of wearing apparel, is chiefly with respect to the flammability, lead, and lead content regulations. It is important pre-importation to verify compliance with CPSC regulations so

---

Box 6.1 Fashion compliance for importers

Factory pre-departure	Product testing
	Complete certifications
	Product labeling
	Origin marking
Pre-arrival to US	Making declarations
	Obtaining other certificates

as to avoid potential problems at the border. In addition, fabrics should always be tested at the outset of a relationship with a new domestic or foreign manufacturer.

Regarding the CPSC's requirements that the GCC "accompany" a shipment, given that US Customs deals physically with cargo and looks for certain records to be included with a shipment, having it both physically contained with the cargo as well as electronically with the other shipping records is a good practice to follow to address the *realities* of facilitating the movement of cargo.

CITES and US fish and wildlife declarations

From python shoes to fur coats, fashion merchandise incorporates animal furs, skins, shells, and other animal by-products across virtually all merchandise categories. Understandably, in order to prevent an excess of capturing and killing animals for these and other commercial purposes, laws have been implemented in an attempt to prevent the extinction of certain animals. The Convention on the International Trade in Endangered Species of Wild Fauna and Flora (CITES) is an international agreement to which over 175 countries have signed. The purpose of this law is to protect almost 35,000 species of animals and plants by ensuring that their international trade is legal and does not threaten their survival in the wild as without regulation, trade has the potential to deplete wildlife populations and lead to extinction.[32] The goal of CITES is to regulate international trade through a series of protocols and prohibitions with respect to animal and plant species as designated across three appendices as follows:

- Appendix I—Species threatened with extinction (provides the greatest level of protection).

- Appendix II—Species that may become threatened with extinction without trade controls, even though they are not currently threatened.

- Appendix III—Species for which countries have requested other member countries help control their international trade.[33]

The US version of CITES is known as the Endangered Species Act (ESA) and it prohibits certain activities with a plant or animal species listed in any of the appendices unless authorized by a permit from the US Fish and Wildlife Service (USFW).[34]

The Endangered Species Act

An **endangered species** is an "animal or plant listed by regulation as being in danger of extinction throughout all or a significant portion of its range."[35] Without a permit, it is unlawful for any person subject to the jurisdiction of the US to

1 import or export an endangered species;

2 harm, harass, pursue, hunt, shoot, trap, collect, or engage in any such related conduct with an endangered species;

3 transport, ship, deliver, carry or receive in foreign or interstate commerce such endangered species; or to

4 offer for sale or sell such endangered species in foreign or interstate commerce.[36]

It would also be a violation of the law where someone attempted to induce another to commit any of the prohibited activities.[37] Imports containing regulated species can clear customs only where a valid CITES permit covering the merchandise has been issued before the import, and the permit itself accompanies the shipment unless a CITES exemption document has been obtained.[38] Due to the commonality of certain goods in the marketplace for which an importer unfamiliar with a product line may not realize that a USFW declaration form may be necessary, such as with a watch containing a mother of pearl shell dial (i.e., the face of the watch), as a rule of thumb, if it involves any animal or plant species, ensuring whether or not this form is required should be done in advance of an import in order to avoid potential delays or even worse, a seizure by CBP of the merchandise at the border.

Record keeping requirements of CBP and CPSC

The proper preparation and maintenance of complete and accurate documentation on all import transactions is essential to both good commercial operations as well as in relation to US Customs compliance. CBP has clear recordkeeping requirements and most of them are the same as those normally kept for business and tax purposes.[39] Records must be kept for five years from the date of entry and be readily available in the event US Customs requests to review an import transaction. Every effort should be made to maintain records on-site going back at least two years, or such longer period as storage will permit. In addition, when records are sent off-site for storage, a log should be kept identifying the records, where they are archived, and how to retrieve them.

CPSC recordkeeping in relation to imports

With regards to what the CPSC requires for records maintenance governing GCCs relating to imports, the GCC itself together with copies of the test results must be kept for three years. Where the importer certifies that the merchandise is compliant with CPSC flammability rules, it must also

1 be in possession of the original, or a copy of, the test certificate upon which the GCC is based; and

2 retain the test certificate together with the original GCC for a minimum of three years after the production date.

Despite the CPSC only requiring a three-year commitment, as they relate to imported merchandise, a good practice would be to keep GCCs with the import records for five years as well.

Principles of fair trade

The concept of **fair trade** is one in which the conditions that facilitate international trade are equitable to all players engaged in the transaction with an emphasis on securing and maintaining (1) the sustainable development of producers supplying goods and (2) the rights, whether economic, social, cultural or otherwise, of those individuals actually providing the labor. The World Fair Trade Organization (WFTO) is a global network of producers, marketers, exporters, importers, wholesalers, and retailers that demonstrate a 100 percent commitment to fair trade and apply the "10 WFTO Principles of Fair Trade" to their supply chain, which range from creating opportunities for economically disadvantaged producers, to demonstrating a respect for the environment.[40]

Ethical fashion in the realm of fair international trade

The WFTO refers to ethical trade as a company's adherence to codes of conduct which ensure that the labor rights of workers are respected. Fair trade goes beyond this and extends to efforts to work in partnership with marginalized and disadvantaged groups to try and help them overcome the serious barriers they face in sustaining livelihoods and finding markets. Therefore, while a fair trade business must be ethical, an ethical business is not necessarily fair trade.[41] The Q&A with Nimet Degirmencioglu (Box 6.2) provides a first-hand look at a fashion company engaged in ethical business practices. As you will read, incorporating fair trade principles into the mission statement of the company can facilitate such implementation into the actual business model.

Box 6.2 Q&A: Interview with Nimet Degirmencioglu, formerly of ethical fashion brand Soham Dave

Nimet Degirmencioglu is a past President of the NYC Fair Trade Coalition, and formerly of the Soham Dave brand. In this Q&A, Nimet shares her wisdom on the operational aspects to maintaining an ethical apparel and accessory brand, and defines what fair trade means to her.

1. How do you define what "fair trade" is?

Fair trade is the open relationship with our artisans and suppliers. Soham Dave promotes local artisans, and fair trade to create a contemporary range of products with an emphasis on biodegradable fabrics, chemical-free dyes, recycled materials, and hand-crafted items. Artisans are the main inspiration for Soham Dave. We want to keep the traditional textiles alive and more importantly innovative.

2. What fair trade principles does Soham Dave follow in its day-to-day business operations?

Creative people should know the materials they are using, where it is coming from, and how it is made. We see the materials and processes that the product is made of as a whole story, and keep the nature, our artisans, and our eco-conscious customer in the heart of Soham Dave. Ethical fashion is growing as consumers are more sensitive about the environment and are demanding more sustainably produced products. Fair trade fits naturally in the way we are doing business. We also follow WFTO principles as a road map. WFTO has the ten fair trade principles stated clearly which is a perfect guideline: http://www.wfto.com/index.php?Itemid=14&id=2&option=com_content&task=view

3. How can a startup implement fair trade practices into its business model?

They should be implemented in the mission statement of the business. More than having a certificate, committing to fair trade is a journey. We are always very open with our transactions. Every decision either finding a production partner or sourcing the materials, can be done using fair trade guidelines.

4. What are some challenges and opportunities to running a fair trade business?

The biggest challenge is updating artisans skills so they can compete in today's market. Communication is another challenge for a fair trade business. You need a partner who can understand the needs and challenges of the artisans and suppliers, and who are also aware of the reality of competing in global markets. You need to create enough market awareness and demand to support your brand.

Resources for more information

US Customs website: www.cbp.gov

CPSC website: www.cpsc.gov

US Fish and Wildlife: www.fws.gov

Key terms

bond	entry filing	tariff
country of origin	fair trade	tariff classification
country of origin of an	Harmonized System	number
apparel or textile	HTSUS number	textile or apparel
product	importer of record	product
customs agency	liquidation	transaction value
customs broker	price paid or payable	ultimate purchaser
customs clearance	protest	US Customs and
customs duties	substantial	Border Protection
endangered species	transformation	wholly assembled

Discussion questions and exercises

1 For countries the US has normal trade relationships with, do their country's imports benefit from the preferential tariff treatment available in the HTSUS? Explain why or why not?

2 For an import to be considered lawfully marked with its country of origin information, what parameters must be met?

3 Distinguish between the FTC's country of origin marking requirement from that of CBP's.

4 Is the transaction value of a shipment simply the invoice value or could there be situations where other costs form a part of the value of imported merchandise? Provide at least two examples of where this type of situation could occur.

5 When would an importer be required to complete a US Fish and Wildlife form on an import of fashion merchandise?

Case study US Customs decisions on conflicting marking

When it comes to clothing and textiles where a brand's trademark or trade name includes words denoting a location which is different from the country of origin itself, US Customs has made decisions as to where and how such country of origin marking may be acceptably done.

One such example is where US Customs dealt with a country of origin question involving the use of the branded "BCBG PARIS" appliqué on an importation of jackets. In its analysis, US Customs recited the FTC's labeling rule as the basis for the jacket being sufficiently labeled, rendering no additional special marking as being necessary. Specifically, it noted that the law ". . . would be satisfied if the jacket containing the registered trademark . . . [was] otherwise properly and conspicuously marked with its country of origin in the inside center of the neck midway between the shoulder seams or in that immediate area . . . On the basis of information described above, we find it unnecessary to require additional country of origin marking on the hangtags containing the trademarks with the non-origin geographical reference. Additionally, the trademark BCBG PARIS appliqués would be considered a decoration and would not reasonably be construed as indicating the country of origin of the submitted jacket sample."[42]

Notes

1. http://otexa.trade.gov/msrcty/v5700.htm (viewed on August 23, 2016).
2. http://www.wcoomd.org/en/about-us/what-is-the-wco/goals.aspx (viewed on August 23, 2016).
3. World Customs Organization Mission, Objectives, Activities, page 2, Nov. 2009 (http://www.wcoomd.org/en/about-us/~/media/WCO/Public/Global/PDF/About%20us/WCO%20In%20Brief/DEPL%20OMD%20UK%20A4.ashx) (viewed on October 9, 2016).
4. https://www.wto.org/english/thewto_e/thewto_e.htm (viewed on August 23, 2016).
5. https://www.wto.org/english/thewto_e/whatis_e/inbrief_e/inbr03_e.htm (viewed on August 23, 2016).
6. https://hts.usitc.gov/current (viewed on August 29, 2016).
7. https://hts.usitc.gov/current (viewed on August 24, 2016).
8. Ibid.
9. https://hts.usitc.gov/current (viewed on August 29, 2016).
10. 19 USC §1304; *Importing into the United States, A Guide for Commercial Importers*, US Customs, last revision 2006.
11. 19 USC §1304.
12. 19 CFR §102.21.
13. 19 CFR §102.21(b)(1).
14. 19 CFR §102.21(b)(6).
15. 19 CFR §134.46.
16. Ibid.
17. Ibid.
18. Ibid.
19. 19 CFR §134.47.
20. Customs Regulations (19 CFR 134.1(b)).
21. *See, United States v. Gibson-Thomsen Co.*, 27 C.C.P.A. 267 (1940); and *National Juice Products Association v. United States*, 628 F. Supp. 978 (Ct. Int'l Trade 1986).
22. 19 USC §1401a.
23. Ibid.
24. 19 USC §1401a(b)(4).
25. 19 USC §1484.
26. 19 CFR §141.0a.
27. 19 CFR §141.0(b) and (d).
28. 19 CFR §159.1.
29. *Importing into the United States, A Guide for Commercial Importers*, US Customs, last revision 2006, page 81.
30. 19 CFR Part 174.

31. Public Law 110–314. 110th Congress.

32. https://www.fws.gov/international/cites/cop16/fws-news-cites–101.pdf (viewed on October 9, 2016).

33. Ibid.

34. https://www.fws.gov/international/pdf/factsheet-endangered-species-act-foreign-species.pdf (viewed on October 9, 2016).

35. Ibid.

36. Ibid.

37. Ibid.

38. CITES Document Requirements, Guidance for US Importers and Exporters.

39. 19 USC §1509(a)(1)(A); 19 CFR Part 163.

40. http://www.wfto.com/about-us/about-wfto (viewed on September 11, 2016).

41. http://www.wfto.com/faq (viewed on September 7, 2016).

42. Customs Ruling Letter N056509 (4/21/09), citing, Customs Headquarters Ruling Letter (HQ) 734455, dated July 1, 1992.

Chapter 7

Exporting for the fashion industry

At the micro level, we see e-commerce sellers offering their merchandise for sale to any purchaser in the world. At the macro level we have seen **reshoring** efforts to bring back manufacturing to the US, including government policies to support increased levels of US exports such as that under former President Obama's 2010 National Export Initiative, which was the first step towards significant changes in US export laws and aimed to rapidly expand industries with high export potential, such as that of the US fashion industry.[1]

Learning objectives

- Understand the process of filing an export declaration
- Recognize when an export of fashion merchandise requires an Automated Export System filing
- Obtain best practices for aligning your website disclosures to successful exporting
- Identify the parties to an export transaction

A rise in an awareness of the importance of reshoring has been especially noticeable in the fashion industry, and particularly so within cities which had enjoyed historical economic prominence thanks to the industry. One such example is that of New York City, where several notable facilities have opened up to support local garment manufacturing and fashion innovation such as the Brooklyn Design + Fashion Accelerator of Pratt College, and Manufacture NY.

An overview of the US export system and process

Any item sent or transported from the US to a foreign destination is an **export**, and whereas shipping one or two pieces of fashion merchandise via an express air courier, such as FedEx or the US Postal Service (USPS) can be relatively straightforward, exporting commercial quantities of goods at higher values can be significantly more complex. Whether a small or large shipment, however, all merchandise being exported is overseen and regulated by the US Department of Commerce (DOC) and its export laws must be adhered to upon the departure of merchandise from the US. As every export has two borders to cross through—that of the US heading outbound, and that of the foreign destination heading inbound to the foreign purchaser—being aware of the import regulations of that foreign country should also be considered when engaging in exporting so as to circumvent any unnecessary delays in delivery of the goods to the buyer.

By definition, selling internationally requires exporting and anyone engaged in this activity is known as an **exporter**. As so many small, medium, and even micro-enterprises are ever increasingly aiming to export, this chapter explains and illustrates which government systems an exporter needs to access and how they can navigate them.

The US Customs "ACE" Portal

US Customs developed an internet accessible platform to connect various government agencies to the international trade community in one centralized place where communications could take place on transactions involving imports and exports. In 2016, CBP mandated the use of this automated commercial environment known as the *ACE Portal* for both importers and exporters and it is within ACE that an export declaration is made.[2]

Making an export declaration

The ACE Portal contains several different linkages to access the various government agencies. With respect to exports, the Automated Export System (AES) and specifically the "AESDirect" platform, is where electronic export information (EEI) is submitted regarding merchandise being exported from the US, Puerto Rico, or the US Virgin Islands.[3] The general rule is that a declaration containing export information must be filed where any product type within a shipment has a value over $2,500 (USD) and must done for every shipment that is exiting the country. It should be noted that the $2,500 amount is not with respect to the total amount of a shipment. Rather, that maximum value is in relation to a specific product type, and therefore where no individual type exceeds $2,500—even where the overall shipment total does—no export declaration is required unless the AES filing is needed for another purpose.

Applying for an exporter account

Making an export declaration requires submitting certain information about the parties involved in the export transaction as well as the products themselves. Much of this information can be obtained from the shipping documents which includes, but is not limited to, the commercial invoice, export shipping instructions, a packing list, and the bill of lading or air waybill.[4] The first step for any exporter is to register as one by creating an exporter account in the ACE system (Figure 7.1). This will grant access to file EEI through AESDirect as well as to initiate the approval process for accessing ACE export reports.

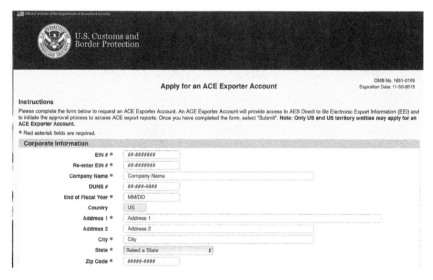

Figure 7.1 US Customs online exporter account form. Source: US Custom and Border Protection.

Timeframes for filing an export declaration

For goods transiting by vessel, including that of fashion merchandise, EEI must be filed in AESDirect and notification to the carrier made twenty-four hours prior to loading the cargo on to the vessel at the US port.[5] When shipping by an air express courier, EEI must be filed and the notification to the courier made no later than two hours prior to the scheduled departure time of the aircraft.[6] Fortunately, as this is typically done by the express courier itself for low valued shipments, this is not ordinarily an area of concern in such circumstance. In addition, an exception to the AES filing exists for low value exports, as discussed at the end of this chapter.

Export data—shipment information

It is important to remember that while the DOC collects export data via the ACE Portal, CBP itself is the agency whose customs agents are actually at the ports monitoring the loading and inspection of cargo on to vessels and airplanes destined to other countries. Such physical oversight is done in tandem with an analysis of the electronic information about the cargo as provided by the exporter or its agent. Submitting accurate data about a shipment to the government is therefore critical, as a failure to do so could lead to a delay in the transport of the exported goods, a fine of up to $10,000, or imprisonment for up to five years for each violation.[7]

The exporter filing identification number

In terms of submitting this data into AESDirect, once an account has been created, an exporter filing identification number is issued which is commonly referred to as the "ITN #." Under this identifier, data related to a shipment is submitted under designated categories which describes the type of merchandise, the parties, and the mode of transportation, as indicated in the "Steps" bar at the top of the AESDirect screen shown in Figure 7.2. It should be noted that many of the selections on this page have a drop down arrow that provides several options and makes the process of completing the filing easier to do as a selection for many of the fields may simply be chosen. All fields with a red star next to the box are required for data submission.

For the party completing the form, otherwise known as the **filer**, the information collected is relatively straightforward as the government simply wants to understand what the cargo is, how it is being transported, and

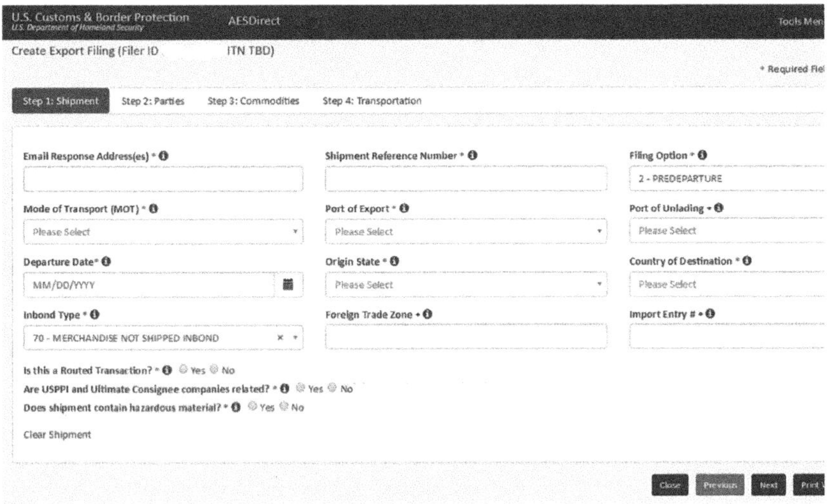

Figure 7.2 Export filing shipment web portal in AESDirect. Source: US Custom and Border Protection.

from where and to whom it is going. Each of these details must be specifically declared. The **port of export** is either the CBP seaport or airport where the goods are loaded on to the aircraft or vessel that is taking the cargo out of the US, or the CBP port where exports by overland transportation cross the US border into Canada or Mexico.[8] The **mode of transportation** is the method by which goods are exported from the US and includes vessel, air, truck, rail, mail or other methods of transport.[9] The **departure date**, or the **date of export**, is the date when the goods are scheduled to leave the port of export on the exporting carrier that is taking the goods out of the US, and the **country of destination** is the country where the goods are to be consumed, further processed, stored, or manufactured.[10] The place where the cargo will be removed from the airplane, vessel, or other mode of transport is known as the **port of unlading**.[11]

Typically for ease of reference, an invoice number is inserted into the field **shipment reference number**, which is a unique identification number assigned to the shipment by the filer for reference purposes.[12] It should be noted that the use of a shipment's reference number is only good once and is prohibited from re-use. As the export declaration should be filed in advance of the export itself, the filing type would ordinarily be one of a "pre-departure" type under this filing option.

The parties to an export transaction

In a traditional sale, we typically think of a single buyer and a single seller. Under the export regulations, a **buyer** is the principal party in the export transaction that purchases the commodities for delivery to the ultimate consignee (defined below), and a **seller** is the principal party in the transaction, who is usually the manufacturer, producer, wholesaler, or distributor of the goods, and who receives the monetary benefit or other consideration for the exported goods.[13]

Principal parties in interest

Since depending on the nature of an export, the party who is the "buyer" or "seller" may not always be clear for purposes of making an export declaration, the export regulations classify them generally as **principal parties in interest**, which are those persons in a transaction that receive the primary benefit, monetary or otherwise, from the transaction.[14]

US principal party in interest

A **US principal party in interest** (USPPI) is the "person or legal entity in the US that receives the primary benefit, monetary or otherwise, from the export transaction. Generally, that person or entity is the US seller, manufacturer, or order party, or the foreign entity while in the US when purchasing or obtaining the goods for export."[15] Under this definition, where a US company is the recipient of a purchase order from an overseas party and invoices them for such exported merchandise, that US company is the USPPI no matter what the terms of sale are, and that entity would appropriately be identified as such in AESDirect (Figure 7.3). Information disclosed about a USPPI would include its tax identification number (as issued by the Internal Revenue Service (IRS)), the company's name, and the contact information of a person at the business.

Foreign principal party in interest

Where a non-US person or entity has purchased the goods for export or is to whom final delivery or end-use of the goods will be made, their information is submitted by the foreign principal party in interest (FPPI) or its agent. It should be noted that an FPPI may also be the **ultimate consignee**,

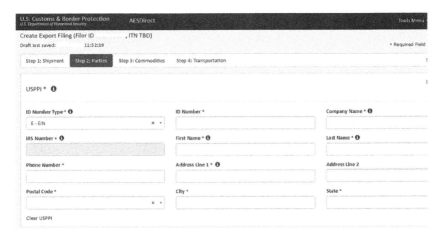

Figure 7.3 AESDirect USPPI web portal. Source: US Custom and Border Protection.

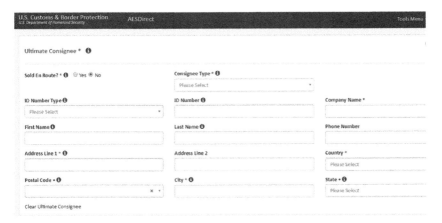

Figure 7.4 Ultimate consignee data portal in AESDirect. Source: US Custom and Border Protection.

which is the person, party, or designee that is located abroad and actually receives the export shipment.[16] Their information must be provided in AESDirect as shown in Figure 7.4, and this is especially important as the US government strictly forbids doing business or engaging in international trade with select individuals, companies, and countries as explained in Chapter 6 on importing.

In addition to an ultimate consignee, in certain transactions there may also be an **intermediate consignee**, which is the person or entity in the foreign country who acts as an agent for the principal party in interest with the purpose of effecting delivery of items to the ultimate consignee.[17] This could be a forwarding agent, bank, or other person who acts as an agent for a principal party in interest.[18] Where such a party is involved in an export transaction, their information must also be provided in AESDirect.

AES filing by an exporter's agent

It would not be uncommon to use a freight forwarder or a forwarding agent to both coordinate the movement of a shipment and do the AES filing on behalf of the USPPI. In fact, this is commonly done in the fashion industry. A **freight forwarder** is broadly defined within the international trade community as a person engaged in the business of assembling, collecting, consolidating, shipping and distributing less than a carload or less than a truckload of freight and who acts as an agent in the trans-shipping of freight to or from foreign countries.[19] For purposes of filing the AES information however, a **forwarding agent** is more narrowly defined as the person in the US authorized by the principal party in interest to facilitate the movement of the cargo from the US to the foreign destination and/or to prepare and file the required documentation.[20] Where an agent is utilized, their identification must be disclosed in AESDirect as shown in Figure 7.5.

Appointing an agent to file EEI

A USPPI may file EEI itself or it can appoint an agent to do so on its behalf.[21] When the USPPI authorizes an agent to file the EEI on its behalf, the export regulations place the responsibility on the USPPI to

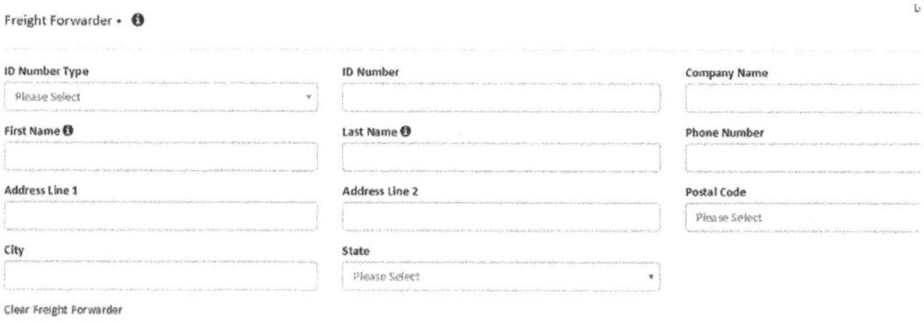

Figure 7.5 Freight forwarder data portal in AESDirect. Source: US Custom and Border Protection.

1 provide its authorized agent with the export information necessary to file the EEI in an accurate and timely manner;

2 retain all documentation needed to support the information provided to the authorized agent for the EEI filing; and

3 obtain a power of attorney or written authorization to file the EEI from the authorized agent.[22]

Importantly, the power of attorney or other written authorization should indicate with specificity the responsibilities of the parties and should state that the agent has been granted the authority to act on behalf of the principal party in interest as its true and lawful agent for purposes of creating and filing EEI in accordance with US laws and regulations.[23]

Agent obligations

The agent, which is often times a freight forwarder, likewise has a series of obligations it must abide by under the export regulations, including:

1 The accurate preparation and timely filing of the EEI based on information received from the USPPI and any other parties involved in the transaction.

2 Obtaining a power of attorney or written authorization from the USPPI to file the EEI and doing so in advance of the first filing.

3 Retaining supporting documentation on the AES reported information.

4 Upon request, providing the USPPI with a copy of the export information filed in a mutually agreed upon format.[24]

In practice, this last requirement can be difficult to enforce where it had not been agreed to at the outset of using an agent. Therefore, when establishing a relationship with an agent, a provision such as this one should be included in a contract entered into for services.

Commodities identification

Once the data about the parties has been submitted, the next step is to provide the details about the merchandise itself. Like imported goods, exports also have a classification number assigned to them in order to identify the type of product being exported from the US. Whether an import classification number or an export one, both are based upon the harmonized tariff system.

Schedule B number

A **Schedule B number** is a ten-digit commodity classification number for exports administered by the DOC's Census Bureau and is the common name for the "Statistical Classification of Domestic and Foreign Commodities Exported from the United States." Schedule B classifications cover everything from live animals and food products to computers and of course, wearing apparel and textiles. Looking up a Schedule B number can be found at the Census Bureau's website at http://www.census.gov/foreign-trade/schedules/b/index.html where a search may be performed for the appropriate commodity classification.

Every AES filing requires the submission of the commodity's Schedule B number together with its description of the exported commodity in English. It must sufficiently describe the commodity to enable the verification of the Schedule B or HTSUS number if ever needed. In addition to this, the quantity of the merchandise, the unit of measure (UOM) (e.g., kilograms), its country of origin, value, and other identifying information must also be disclosed (Figure 7.6).

Country of origin

It should be noted that just because a product is being exported from the US does not automatically mean that its origin is American. This is because goods imported into the US do not automatically lose their origin identification

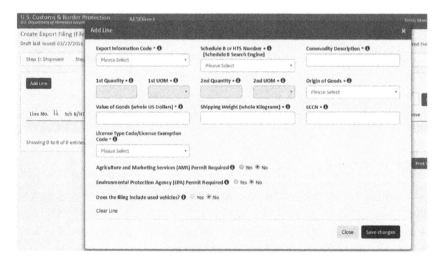

Figure 7.6 Schedule B data portal in AESDirect. Source: US Custom and Border Protection.

based on the fact that they may be currently located in America. An example of this would be where a US retailer has imported a large quantity of wearing apparel from one country and is reselling a portion of it, without having made any improvements to the garments, to a foreign buyer. Since the product originated from another country, the identification that the export is "foreign" would be indicated in AESDirect to denote that it had previously been imported and though stored in the US, had not actually been subject to any **enhancement**, which is defined in the export regulations to mean a change or modification to a good which increases its value or improves its condition.[25] In fact, for export purposes, a **domestic export** is comprised of only such goods that are grown, produced, or manufactured in the US along with commodities of foreign origin that have been changed in the US from the form in which they were imported.[26]

Transportation information

Data relevant to the mode of transportation is the last set of data to provide in AESDirect. It includes information about the carrier itself, each of which is designated its own unique identifier known as the Standard Carrier Alpha Code (SCAC) for vessel, rail, and truck shipments or the International Air Transport Association (IATA) code for air shipments. This carrier identification is input into the "Carrier SCAC/IATA" field (Figure 7.7) to specify the carrier transporting the cargo out of the US.

It should be noted that the carrier identification is not always required, even where the shipment is over $2,500. Examples of this include when shipped via USPS or being transported via passenger hand carried language.[27] Lastly, there

Figure 7.7 Transportation data portal in AESDirect. Source: US Custom and Border Protection.

is a field referred to as the "Transportation Reference Number" (TRN), which is optional for cargo carried by air, rail or truck.[28] For ocean-borne vessel shipments, however, it is a mandatory disclosure and the **booking number**, which is the reservation number assigned by a carrier to hold space on the vessel for cargo being exported, is what is required to be reported in AESDirect.[29] As this is the last step in the AES filing process, upon the successful transmission of data the filer is issued a confirmation, and a summary of the EEI is available for review.

Additional AES filing requirements and exceptions

In accordance with US export regulations, whether filing it itself or using a freight forwarder or other agent, the USPPI or its agent is required to:[30]

1 File complete and accurate information in a timely manner.

2 Respond to errors, warnings, verify and reminder messages, and compliance alerts generated by the AES.

3 Provide the exporting carrier with the required proof of filing citations.

4 Promptly file corrections or cancellations to EEI.

5 Retain all necessary and proper documentation related to EEI transactions.

In order to file EEI in AESDirect, the USPPI or its filing agent must first be certified to do so which would denote that party's authorization to transmit and receive data from AES, and their agreement to comply with all export rules and regulations issued by the various government agencies.[31]

An exception to filing EEI: E-commerce exports of low value

An exception to filing EEI exists where a shipment contains merchandise which has a value under $2,500, as is typical with fashion products sold on an e-commerce platform. The exception is applicable when merchandise is shipped from one USPPI to one consignee, transported on a single exporting carrier, and is classified under a single Schedule B number. An example of this would be where an e-commerce store sells a cashmere sweater for $250 to an individual buyer and the shipment is being transported by plane to a destination outside of the US via express courier FedEx.

Utilizing the United States Postal Service for exporting

Sellers of low value goods, as many e-commerce fashion sellers are, often utilize the United States Postal Service (USPS) for shipping their merchandise. When shipping to most locations outside of the US, the completion of a customs form is required, which can either be done at the post office or online at www.usps. com. This form advises the destination country what the products contained within the package are together with its dutiable value. When shipping under USPS options, there are different customs forms which may be used, such as with their express options like Global Express Guaranteed®. A customs form is not required, however, if the package is going by First Class Mail International® or when a seller is using a USPS Priority Mail International Flat Rate™ envelope.[32] The USPS website is equipped with plenty of information to help take the guesswork out of customs forms, so be sure to reference it when shipping with this mode of transportation.

Exports transit through two borders

Recognizing that there are two borders through which a shipment must cross, it is important to remember that customs duties are regularly assessed on shipments imported into other countries by the foreign customs agency. All items entering a foreign country are subject to inspection by the customs agency, and the payment of duties and taxes in accordance with that country's national laws may be required.

Record-keeping requirements for exporters

All documents pertaining to an export shipment must be kept for five years from the date of export. In addition, it is mandatory that anyone who has received a certification notice approving them to file through AESDirect keep this record for as long as they continue to submit EEI through AESDirect.[33]

Preparing a product's webpage for shipping to foreign destinations

Foreign purchasers new to buying from the US may not know about the additional duties, taxes or other fees that may be assessed against them by their own country's customs authorities when trying to retrieve their package from their local post office or other pick up location. Therefore, because delays and duty payments may arise, best practices for website disclaimers are that they are conspicuously placed on a website to alert buyers to this. Some best practices include disclaimers that:

- Additional payments to the government (and not to the seller) of customs duties, taxes or other fees, may be required in order to collect the package.
- The seller will make a reasonable effort to resolve delivery delays.
- Despite its best effort to reasonably resolve delivery delays, the seller is not responsible for shipment delays to countries outside of the US due to customs related issues in the foreign country.
- Where unforeseen delays may occur it could result in the package being delivered past thirty days of purchase.

By including these statements, a seller has now provided a reasonable basis as required by the FTC for stating or implying that a product may not be able to be shipped within the timeframe represented on the website. Additional information on FTC marketing statements may be found in Chapter 4.

Best practices for completing the export declaration on e-commerce sales

Accurate product information is critical for minimizing delays of a shipment entering a foreign country. The foreign customs authorities will need to have clear information on what the product is so that it can assess duties on the value of the good if required, along with the true country of origin identified to streamline a shipment's entry. Some recommendations for aligning website descriptions for export declaration purposes include:

- Stating accurate product descriptions on the webpage, e.g.; 95% cotton / 5% spandex women's t-shirt (copy and paste this information directly into the international shipping label).
- Stating the value at which the product was *actually* sold versus a pre-sale price (e.g., if coupons used).
- Asking foreign buyers to re-write in the "comments to seller" box their address the way it is typically written in their country, so that all address data points are in their proper place.

- If selling samples, state on both the (a) web page description and (b) on the shipping label, that the shipment contains a "SAMPLE."[34]

By following these best practices, sellers can minimize confusion and avoid the stress that arises from delayed shipments, whether brought on by a distressed customer or a government regulatory authority.

Resources for more information

USPS Global Express Guaranteed Service Guide: http://about.usps.com/ publications/pub141/welcome.htm

Logistics Overview by Export.gov https://www.export.gov/logistics

Key terms

booking number	exporter	principal parties in
buyer	filer	interest
carrier identification	forwarding agent	reshoring
country of	freight forwarder	schedule B number
destination	intermediate	seller
date of export	consignee	shipment reference
departure date	mode of	number
domestic export	transportation	ultimate consignee
enhancement	port of export	US principal party in
export	port of unlading	interest

Discussion questions and exercises

1. Must the principal party in interest be based in the US or can it be a foreign company? Under what circumstances could it be the latter and what are they called?

2. If an exporter wanted to use a freight forwarder to file its AES EEI, what would it need to obtain in advance of the first exported shipment?

3. What is the purpose of the Schedule B number?

Box 7.1 Top five areas to consider when going global, by Irving Williamson, former chairman of the USITC

Irving Williamson* served as a Commissioner to the US International Trade Commission (USITC) for several years in addition to presiding as its Chairman. The USITC is responsible for implementing and updating the HTSUS and integrating negotiated trade agreements into practical application. He lends his advice here giving us his top five list of factors to consider for expanding to foreign markets.

1   Before thinking of going global, any business should ask itself the following questions: Are we successful in our home market? Did we develop and execute successfully a business plan for our home market? Are our near and intermediate prospects in the home market secure enough that we can devote resource to entering a foreign market?

2   There are times you may have a product (either merchandise or a service) or be engaged in a line of business for which the international market is much more attractive than the domestic market, but most often your success in your home market is an indication to both yourself and your customers that you know your business well enough that you may be successful internationally.

3   Is there a demand in a particular foreign market for my particular product or service? If you are thinking about importing a product or service, you must ask if there is demand in a particular home market for it. Of course, this assessment must be backed up with good market research.

4   Before doing extensive research on the market, you need to consider whether you have the skills and experience to operate in the relevant market to which you want to sell or from which you want to procure goods and services. Do you know the language, do you understand the culture and the local business practices? Do you have particular contacts with reliable suppliers and distributors in the foreign market you want to sell into or source from?

5   If the foregoing questions can be answered affirmatively, then you need to ask what are the applicable regulations that would affect the ability to import or export the product or to engage in the service and if there are, can you comply with them in a way that will not undermine the viability of your business? Second, are there foreign or US regulatory barriers that affect your product, unusually high tariffs or fees, licensing or customs

procedures that are so arbitrary or non-transparent that even the most diligent have trouble negotiating them? What is the business climate and do you have the resources and skill to deal with it if it is unfavorable? You can answer yourself if there are trade agreements in existence or coming into existence that address some of the barriers you have identified, and, if so, what are the chances that you can successfully take advantage of them? (This must be a tough-minded assessment since, unless you are in the business of government relations and fighting with governments or can afford to hire someone who is, the risk that your efforts may not succeed or may be too costly, may be too great.)

If you can answer the foregoing questions affirmatively, then it is time to draw up a business plan and go forth.

* Irving Williamson has fifty years of international trade experience, including as a Foreign Service Officer, a Deputy General Counsel at the Office of the US Trade Representative, head of his own trade policy consulting firm and, since 2007, as a Commissioner at the US International Trade Commission where he served as Chairman from 2012 to 2014. The views expressed in the interview are his own personal views and not those of the US International Trade Commission.

Notes

1. http://trade.gov/nei/ (viewed on September 24, 2016).
2. https://www.cbp.gov/trade/automated/getting-started/using-ace-secure-data-portal (viewed on September 17, 2016).
3. 15 CFR §30.1.
4. Ibid.
5. 15 CFR §30.4(b)(1).
6. 15 CFR §30.4(b)(2).
7. 15 CFR §30.71(a).
8. 15 CFR §30.1.
9. Ibid.
10. Ibid.
11. Ibid.
12. Ibid.
13. Ibid.
14. Ibid.
15. Ibid.
16. Ibid.

17. Ibid.
18. Ibid.
19. Hinkelman, Edward *Dictionary of International Trade*, 6th edition, World Trade Press p. 85, 2005.
20. 15 CFR §30.1.
21. 15 CFR §30.5(c).
22. Ibid.
23. 15 CFR §30.3(f).
24. 15 CFR §30.3(c)(2).
25. 15 CFR §30.1.
26. Ibid.
27. 15 CFR §30.6(a)(8).
28. 15 CFR §30.6(a)(14)(i)–(iv).
29. 15 CFR §30.6(a)(14)(i).
30. 15 CFR §30.3(d)(3).
31. 15 CFR §30.5(d).
32. https://www.usps.com/international/customs-forms.htm (viewed on September 24, 2016).
33. 15 CFR §30.10(a)(2).
34. Even if a sample is not intended for resale it can nonetheless have a value, so be sure that an accurate value is provided even if it is a low one.

Chapter 8

Working with logistics and transportation providers

Like any purchase that requires a delivery, having great customer service, secure packaging, and quick—or at least reliable—shipping makes a buyer both satisfied with the shopping experience as well as eager to buy from the seller again. As such, whether selling clothing, accessories, or footwear, creating this experience for new and repeat customers is essential, and to the extent the goods you sell are imported, it is critical that your inventory arrive in pristine condition ready for the sales floor or further distribution.

Learning objectives

- Gain packaging strategies to reduce costs and create a streamlined marketing look
- Distinguish freight forwarder services from those of transportation providers
- Understand how, when, and why to obtain cargo insurance

Reliable transportation is important not only for the protection of goods in transit but also to protect the "bottom line" of wholesalers and importers. This is because some retailers impose severe penalties on a seller who delivers late or otherwise causes a shipment to be considered a misdelivery. This can occur for several reasons, such as that a delivery was made to the wrong store location, or that the merchandise received was in the wrong color, style, size, or was otherwise nonconforming. Some types of punitive measures that a retailer may impose include

- refusing to accept and pay for a late shipment;
- assessing a fee for the late delivery, or a failure to deliver conforming goods (also known as a **chargeback**); or
- ceasing to have any further business relationship with a seller.

To avoid these issues, it is critical to know your supply chain, instruct suppliers on packing protocols to ensure the secure transportation and delivery to you or your customer's location, and to be aware of any shipping delays so that customers and other key stakeholders may be notified accordingly.

Planning the journey

Transporting fashion merchandise from one location to another can be as simple as dropping off a package containing a pair of shoes at a UPS® store and awaiting the confirmation email of its delivery, or a quick check through their website's tracking portal. Larger shipments however, can take on added complexity due to the documentation involved, the distance traveled, and the risks that accompany the journey. Take, for example, an imported shipment of wearing apparel transported across the high seas in an ocean container vessel. Coordination with third parties may include, but is not limited to:

- Providing trucking services from the foreign factory to the foreign port.
- Clearing the export with the foreign customs authority.
- The physical carriage of the ocean-borne shipment.
- Obtaining US Customs clearance upon arrival to the US.
- Delivery to the final purchaser and/or warehouse.

All of these steps may be coordinated by the shipper itself. More commonly, however, is to hire a third party well-versed in a particular foreign market, or who works in tandem with one. This is because they know who the trustworthy service providers are, the local language and customs, and can readily coordinate all of the parties needed to facilitate the movement and export clearance of the merchandise. Prior to any transport, however, merchandise must be properly packaged and prepared for the actual journey and this is where advanced planning can make the difference between a shipment that arrives intact versus damaged or destroyed.

Preparing your cargo for shipping: Packaging integrity

Proper packaging is critical to ensure the quality and integrity of shipped goods. Not only must the exterior packaging be secure, but it must be able to sustain the avoidance of problems such as pests, e.g., moths getting into a shipment of wool sweaters destined for a retailer. The damage that would ensue is not only to the clothing, but also to the relationship between the shipper and purchaser who is relying on the arrival of goods in excellent condition rather than a shipment of damaged goods which cannot be sold. In addition, packaging needs to be of such a caliber to prevent damages that may arise for reasons beyond a shipper's control. An example of this would be where a shipment of denim jeans are loaded into a metal shipping container for vessel transport. Due to several trips across the high seas, rust and corrosion on the container have led to small holes in its exterior leading to a compromise in its structure. The result is that water seepage occurs and instead of an order of merchandise arriving ready for the sales floor, a container of moldy and mildewed jeans is delivered. For reasons such as these, taking advance precautions to use appropriate packaging or conducting a pre-shipping inspection of a container can prove to be prudent measures and should be considered with every shipment.

Shipping container integrity

The overseas or overland transport of large shipments raise separate risk issues from that of the small package. This is often times due to the distance traveled, as the more time needed, the more opportunities there are for the integrity of the packaging to be compromised by unforeseen events. Where a shipper has an opportunity to send an entire container load of goods, it would be wise to instruct the seller to perform an empty container inspection for any damage, paying special attention to factors such as

- the existence of a parasitic device inside (to prevent pests);
- that the rivets on the exterior door locking mechanism are in good condition; and
- to look for any evidence of welding marks or other repair inside the container or around the rivets.

Packaging for omni-channel distribution

Retailers that operate both stores and websites encourage shopping across channels so that purchasers will shop both online and in stores. Known as **omni-channel** retailing, package design considerations for logistics purposes should be thought of pre-production to achieve a consistent presentation in relation to the branding of goods bought through either channel, as explained by Chad Schofield of logistics company BoxC in the Q&A at the end of this chapter (Box 8.3). **Logistics** is "the process of planning, implementing and controlling the flow of personnel, materials and information from the point of origin to the point of destination at the required time and in the desired condition."[1] Whether it is a factor such as the dimensional weight which impacts shipping costs (as smaller packages cost less to ship), or a design aesthetic where arriving packages can go from crate to shelf, advance planning between the marketing and transportation departments can lead to overall cost savings and potentially improve efficiencies.

Packaging to expedite the process of transportation to the sales floor

As in all businesses, identifying ways to improve and streamline processes are always desired. Merchandise preparedness to expedite the unloading of cargo from a shipping container to the sales floor is one such method that can achieve this, as companies can instruct that their goods be packaged in a particular way to facilitate this. For example, instructions may be provided to a shipper to prepare garments as hanging on hangers, folded and wrapped in plastic bags, or in several other configurations depending on the article itself.

In addition to instructing a supplier, the use of a third party to provide specific sorting, packaging, and other services to aid in the organization of garments for retail sale and distribution is also commonly used in the fashion industry. To illustrate this, take the example of a company selling children's sleepwear which ships a container load of its merchandise to a warehouse that provides sorting and repackaging services. These may include the unsealing and unstrapping of cartons so that garments can be unpacked and pressed, placed on hangers, wrapped with tissue paper, placed in polybags, and repacked for retail sale in boxes containing a select number of garments. Services from a third-party warehouse could also include the installation of cartons into a shipping container in a specific configuration in order to minimize wasted container space and freight charges, or the packing of cartons on to pallets, which may decrease the time spent loading the goods and handling the containers.

Packaging tips when selling a small order directly to a customer

Purchasing standard shipping envelopes and boxes, or using those provided by USPS or an express courier, are simple ways to ship small quantities of merchandise. The materials are readily available, often times free of charge when using one of these service providers, and can be picked up at the same location from which the goods are shipped.

When it comes to fashion merchandise, while corrugated boxes or paper mailers would typically provide adequate protection in most weather scenarios, it is the prevention against water damage that prompts the use of some type of plastic packaging for the transport of goods, whether in the form of a plastic wrap on the interior, or use of a bubble mailer as the shipping envelope itself. Irrespective of the type used, because unknown events can always occur, the option to insure cargo is always available and should periodically be considered.

Insuring the cargo

When making a purchase, cargo insurance may be automatically included as a result of the shipping type chosen, such as in the case of USPS Priority Mail®. Alternatively, a customer may opt to purchase it. When transporting a large order of inventory to a retail store, the onus would typically be on the purchaser as a customer of the distributor's or importer's to buy insurance. After all, while a weathered and damaged cargo container may make a terrific background for a photo shoot like in the image in Figure 8.1, as illustrated in the moldy blue jeans example above the risks associated with the transportation of merchandise in a rusty or otherwise

Figure 8.1 Rusty containers work for a photo shoot but not for apparel transport. Source: iStock.com/freemixer.

deteriorating cargo container can lead to damage in the tens of thousands of dollars or more.

Unforeseen events can and do occur

Perhaps less frequently asked than it should be is the question of: "What would I do if my shipment were damaged, lost, stolen or mishandled?" From incidents of severe weather where a container may be tossed into the sea, to that of broken machinery handling the loading of the container on to or off of the vessel, to contamination or infiltration of the container itself, unforeseen events can and do occur, and protection against these costly events is obtained through the purchase of cargo insurance. Like most insurance policies, the party purchasing the insurance policy is known as the **insured** and a policy is typically bought to cover the equivalent of the value of the subject merchandise. Where an incident occurs for which the insured has suffered damages, such as the cost of the mildewed jeans in the above example, the insured would file a claim with the insurance company seeking payment equivalent to the value of the lost cargo. Depending on the level of coverage bought, an amount often times must be paid in advance by the insured prior to the remainder of the claim being paid, which is known as the **deductible**. To avoid paying a deductible, which could be $500 for example, an insured may elect to pay a higher **premium**, which is the cost of the policy itself, at the outset in order to have a zero dollar deductible.

The role of the transportation intermediary

With nearly one-third of all merchandise imported into the US being that of wearing apparel and textiles, it follows that most of it arrives to the US by vessel as air transportation is significantly more expensive. Ocean-borne transport is regulated by the **Federal Maritime Commission** (FMC), which is the US government agency that has regulatory oversight of vessels transiting the ports of the US. It is responsible for setting the rules and regulations of those operating in the maritime industry, including those of vessel-operating common carriers, such as the cargo container lines like Maersk®. The FMC also regulates what are known as **ocean transportation intermediaries** (OTIs) which can be either a non-vessel-operating common carrier, commonly referred to as an NVOCC or NVO, or an "ocean freight forwarder," each of which is defined in Table 8.1.

Table 8.1 Ocean transportation intermediaries (OTIs) defined[2]

Ocean freight forwarder	Means a person who
	• dispatches shipments from the US via a common carrier,
	• books or otherwise arranges space for those shipments on behalf of shippers, and
	• may collect, consolidate, ship and distribute less than container loads of freight.[3]
	It may also process the documentation or perform related activities incident to those shipments.
Non-vessel-operating-common carrier (NVOCC)	means a common carrier
	• which does not operate the vessels by which the ocean transportation is provided, and
	• is a shipper in its relationship with an ocean common carrier.

The distinctions between a freight forwarder and an NVOCC are important to note as interactions with such parties will likely rise as the volume of merchandise a company ships grows. The two OTIs are further important to understand as the liability of either of these service providers in relation to any unforeseen damage to transported cargo can change depending on their role as a freight forwarder versus that of an NVOCC.

Freight forwarder services

Freight forwarder services refers to the dispatching of shipments on behalf of others in order to facilitate the transportation by a common carrier.[4] Services can range from preparing and processing export documents, including the required electronic export information (*see* Chapter 7 on exports), to giving expert advice to exporters concerning letters of credit, licenses, other documents, or inspections.[5] Other services a freight forwarder may provide include, but are not limited to, those listed in Box 8.1.

Box 8.1 Freight forwarder services[6]

- Booking, arranging for or confirming cargo space.

- Preparing and/or processing common carrier bills of lading or other shipping documents.

- Arranging for cargo insurance.

- Arranging for warehouse storage.

- Assisting with clearing shipments in accordance with government regulations.

- Coordinating the movement of shipments from origin to vessel.

- Preparing and/or sending advance notifications of shipments or other documents to banks, shippers, or consignees, as required.

The freight forwarder as a travel agent

By way of analogy, a freight forwarder can be thought of as playing a role similar to one a travel agent would play to those seeking to have a vacation planned and booked by a third party. It literally plans out the travel of a shipment's voyage. Where the freight forwarder is also a licensed US Customs broker (*see* Chapter 6 on imports), the clearance of the merchandise through US Customs, i.e., the filing of the entry and payment of customs duties, may also be performed by the same entity on behalf of the importer. While the carriage of goods may be booked directly with a common carrier itself, it will more likely be done with an NVOCC or a freight forwarder.

Non-vessel-operating common carrier (NVOCC) services

To the average person, an NVOCC often appears to be the carrier itself even though in reality it is not. This is because they do not actually have their own vessels but instead purchase transportation services from a vessel-operating common carrier and then resell such service at a higher rate to shippers in either single containers or **consolidated containers**, which is where a shipping container holds the packages of multiple shippers. Similar to a freight forwarder, an NVOCC works to coordinate the movement of the cargo as needed by a shipper, and typically issues its own **contract of carriage**, which is a contract for the transport of freight.[7] The NVOCC is, therefore, acting as an intermediary between the customers who are shipping the goods and the vessel steamship lines. Services provided by an NVOCC may include, but are not limited to:[8]

1 Coordinating the movement of shipments between origin or destination and vessel.

2 Arranging for inland transportation and paying for inland freight charges where the transportation continues on land once offloaded from the vessel.

3 Payment of port-to-port or multimodal transportation charges.

4 The payment of compensation to ocean freight forwarders.

Shipper

Where an NVOCC is used, the way in which a shipper may be defined can become confusing as the NVOCC itself becomes the shipper in relation to the vessel common carrier. For this reason, a shipper can be defined as having several identities, including that of a cargo owner, the person for whose account the ocean transportation is provided or to whom delivery is to be made, or an NVOCC that accepts responsibility for payment of all applicable charges.[9]

As explained above, the nuances as to who is considered the shipper becomes relevant in relation to a damaged shipment. For this reason, irrespective of the type of fashion merchandise being shipped, it is important to understand which title and its corresponding definition a party actually falls into as the ability to recover money for damaged goods is often determined by this.

Obtaining price quotes on a shipment

Depending on the volume of merchandise, a price quote may be obtained under several methods. In the case of an express courier, for certain package sizes it simply has a fixed price that the shipper is subject to paying which includes the cost of shipping along with any other optional or mandatory service that may be provided, such as a confirmation of delivery. For larger shipments being transported by vessel however, the cost to ship may be dependent upon the transportation provider's **tariff**, which is the price set by a carrier for the transport of goods and includes the actual rates, charges, classifications, rules, regulations and practices of a common carrier or a group of related ones. In the context of transportation, the word tariff should not to be confused with that of a customs *tariff classification number*, as described in Chapter 6.

Modes of transport

Irrespective of whether it is footwear, apparel, accessories, or any other type of goods, where moving by airplane, truck, ship, or train, a contract of carriage will be involved that lays out some basic information about the sender, receiver, and the cargo itself. For international shipments, it would also include details such as the foreign port of export, and the arriving port of import. Being a transportation contract, there would also be terms and conditions that the carrier would subject a party using their service to agree to, including what is known as a **limitation of liability** that the carrier uses to limit the amount of money it would be required to pay in the event a shipment got lost, was stolen, or arrived in damaged condition.

Transportation by vessel

The fashion industry depends on the reliable transportation of cargo containers across the high seas for the delivery of shipments to the US. Most, if not all, vessel carriers have a sailing schedule which provides a reasonable assurance that cargo departing from a particular port will arrive on a specific date at its destination. The contract of carriage for a vessel shipment is known as a **bill of lading**, which is a document of title acknowledging the receipt of goods by a carrier or by the shipper's agent.[10] It establishes the pricing and terms of the contract between a shipper and the transportation company, is proof that the carrier is in receipt of the goods described in the bill of lading, contains the details pertaining to the terms under which the freight is to be moved, and specifies the locations from which the goods are to be transported to and from.

It further serves as a document of **title**, i.e., legal ownership, and therefore when a buyer goes to pick up their merchandise, providing an original copy of the bill of lading is normally required so that the carrier can confirm that the party picking up the goods actually has the legal authority to do so.

Value limits under COGSA

As explained above, while using seaworthy containers is one of the core concerns to be aware of, it is also important to recognize—especially for those *not* obtaining cargo insurance—that the terms and conditions in the bill of lading of several ocean common carriers limit their transportation liability to $500 per package. That is, where cargo has not been insured but is damaged while in the custody of the carrier, unless the number of packages had been declared and additional sums paid for such enumerated packages in advance of the issuance of the bill of lading, the party seeking to recover monies for damaged cargo will likely only be allowed to recover the maximum amount of $500 per "package," with the number of packages being determined by the carrier. This blanket rule stems from a law commonly referred to as COGSA, which stands for the Carriage of Goods by Sea Act.[11] For goods in transit by vessel, COGSA defines the rights and responsibilities of issuers and holders of ocean bills of lading.[12] It is within these rules that carriers create their own terms and conditions, including those with respect to filing a claim with it for damaged cargo.

Filing a claim with a carrier

It is important to pay attention to the provisions in a bill of lading regarding notices to the carrier when making a claim of cargo damage, loss, misdelivery, or otherwise. It is critical that any notice be made following the steps required by the carrier as the viability for collecting on a cargo loss or damage claim will rest on having notified the carrier in writing of such claim within a certain time period, such as within six weeks, of discovering the damage. A failure to have performed this notification could be used as a bar by the transportation provider to pay out any monies owed. As this is a pre-requisite under most ocean vessel contracts, it is important to understand how and by when to notify a carrier in order to preserve your claim. Given the prevalence of digital documentation in the maritime industry today, where you are considering working with a particular carrier, or where you have already started to but have never seen its terms and conditions, which traditionally were printed on the back of the bill of lading, be sure to specifically request from the carrier a copy of their terms so that an awareness of any activities you may be required to undertake are known.

Transportation by air

Moving cargo by air is expensive when you compare it to vessel transportation, however whereas two weeks may be required for the arrival of a container ship, the same distance may be traveled by airplane in less than twenty-four hours. For smaller packages and those needed quickly, air travel is the obvious mode of transport. The contract of carriage for shipments transported by air is known as the **air waybill**. The airline industry has a standard version of an air waybill that it has adopted for both domestic and international travel. The limitations of liability can nonetheless vary from carrier to carrier, and should therefore be reviewed in advance of any shipment.

Transportation by truck or rail

While the transport of fashion merchandise over land by truck or rail does occur from the neighboring countries of Canada and Mexico, it is also common that clothing and accessories arriving from foreign ports continue their journey by these modes of transportation to their final destination. While individually rail carriers and trucks have their own contracts of carriage, where the journey continues from an ocean carrier such transportation may instead be organized under an intermodal transportation contract of carriage. Irrespective of how the rail or truck journey is routed however, where a **rail waybill** is issued, that is the freight document that indicates goods have been received for shipment by rail,[13] or a **trucker's bill of lading** for domestic shipments by truck, attention should be paid to the terms and conditions for the limitations of liability along with that carrier's specific requirements for certain activities, such as reporting a misdelivery or an incident involving damaged cargo, for the same reasons stated above in relation to preserving claims under an ocean bill of lading.

Incoterms

Globally there is a common "language" that governs the transportation of international shipments. Known as **Incoterms**, they are a series of standardized shipping terms defined by the International Chamber of Commerce, which apportions the costs and liabilities of international shipping between buyers and sellers. These shipping terms are typically referred to as three letter acronyms that indicate the obligations, risks, and costs of both the seller and buyer involving the transportation and delivery of goods, and can apply to either an import or export. Published by the International Chamber of Commerce (ICC), the 2010 version of Incoterms have their meaning provided in Box 8.2.

Box 8.2 Incoterms[14]

Transportation by water

CIF	Cost, Insurance, and Freight
CFR	Cost and Freight
FAS	Free Alongside Ship
FOB	Free on Board

Transportation by any mode

CIP	Carriage and Insurance Paid to
CPT	Carriage Paid To
EXW	Ex Works
DAP	Delivered at Place
DAT	Delivered at Terminal
DDP	Delivered Duty Paid
FCA	Free Carrier

Incoterms relate to common sales practices and are particularly important with overseas shipments as a misunderstanding as to a term's application could render a party responsible for shipping or other costs which it may have sought to avoid. Examples include, being liable for the payment of damage to merchandise that occurs during transportation, not obtaining title to the goods at the place and time that had been expected, or discovering the cost of shipping the goods was incorrectly calculated when placing the order. More information on Incoterms may be found at www.iccwbo.org.

Key terms

air waybill	deductible	instrument of
bill of lading	Federal Maritime	international
chargeback	Commission	traffic
consolidated	freight forwarder	insured
containers	services	limitation of liability
contract of carriage	Incoterms	logistics

non-vessel-operating	ocean transportation	rail waybill
common carrier	intermediary	tariff
(NVOCC)	omni-channel	title
ocean freight forwarder	premium	trucker's bill of lading

Discussion questions and exercises

1 Describe the differences between freight forwarder services and those of a non-vessel-operating common carrier.

2 What are some methods that can be used to improve efficiencies and streamline the process of shipping merchandise to be sales floor ready?

3 When performing a shipping container examination, what factors should be paid special attention to during an inspection to verify its structural integrity?

4 Describe your own experience using a logistics provider, taking an example of a product that you received or sent using a courier such as FedEx® or another service provider.

Case study Target's recyclable hanger program and the treatment of hangers as instruments of international traffic[15]

When it comes to global shipping and cost savings, it would be wise to look at the total life cycle of the merchandise and its containers or holders being imported and not merely the merchandise in isolation. It is not uncommon to find hangers being used in the transport of apparel, and when it comes to the payment of US Customs duties (*see* Chapter 6), the question has arisen as to whether it is classifiable as part of the garment itself, or if it can be designated as an instrument of international traffic.

Target Corporation ("Target") is a US-based mass-market retailer which implemented a hanger recycling program with Braiform

Industries ("Braiform"), a manufacturer and recycler of hangers for re-use. These hangers were sturdy and capable of re-use, potentially up to four times, and arrived to the US hanging imported garments transported from foreign manufacturers to Target's retail stores. Once an article was sold, the hangers were collected for recycling, and thereafter shipped to Braiform for which annual estimates of returned hangers exceeded 200 million hangers that were recycled through this program. As this program was doing a lot of good for the environment, Target sought a determination by US Customs that these hangers qualified as an **instrument of international traffic**, which requires an article to be

- used as a container or holder;
- be substantial;
- be suitable for and capable of repeating use; and
- used in significant numbers in international traffic.

Target sought this determination because with it, the payment of customs duties on the value of the hangers would not be required. Fortunately, due to the hanger's "relatively durable construction," US Customs concluded that they were a type that was physically capable of being re-used in international traffic and ultimately, not subject to any duty payments. This decision was, therefore, a win for both Target's bottom line as well as the environment.

Box 8.3 Logistics considerations for the shipping of fashion merchandise, by Chad Schofield, CoFounder and CDO at the logistics company, BoxC

The problem with logistics, is it's an afterthought.

Packaging should be designed from the beginning with logistics in mind in addition to presentation and brand identity. By designing packaging with logistics in mind from the beginning a consistent presentation can be achieved for omni-channel distribution and save money by minimizing dimensional weight issues.

As omni-channel distribution, that is retail stores and online, is effectively the standard, thought should be given to how the presentation can be completely different between the two retail channels. Packaging should be designed to deliver a delightfully packaged dress received in the mail undamaged without adding much weight or bulk but also making it easy for a boutique to unpack and hang on the racks without much waste.

With clothing there is usually not many instances when dimensional weight is a problem but with shoes the design of shoe boxes almost always creates a problem with dimensional weight. Pushing a shoebox designer to make the box as small as possible will save money with shipping no matter which transportation mode.

It should be noted that dimensional weight has always been the chargeable weight for international shipments but domestically this is now also the case, except with USPS.

Practice safe addressing! The most common problem with lost or late delivery of orders is preventable! It is worth every penny to use an address verification service during the online checkout which requires the addressee to enter a correct address.

And related to lost and late deliveries, there is a growing consensus building with all online retailers that logistics should be moved, at least partially, to the marketing department from the operations department. The reasoning is that late, damaged, or lost orders sent by post or courier are a drain on customer service resources and reflect badly on the brand. An order that arrives on time or early and undamaged is a delight for a customer. Alternatively, an order that is delivered late and/or damaged is a disappointment for a customer. To delight customers more, orders should be packed with presentation in mind. And to turn a customer into a fan, include a little extra surprise with the order.

There's not much difference between air freight and sea freight operationally. The difference is cost and time. Sea freight is cheap but typically has a 21–30 day delivery time. Air freight is expensive but typically has a 3–7 day delivery time. The one exception to this rule of thumb is "less than container" shipments, shipments that do not fill a forty foot shipping container. If a shipment would fill only about 25 percent of a shipping container then it can become more cost effective to ship by air freight because of the fixed charges of sea freight.

Notes

1. Hinkelman, Edward, *Dictionary of International Trade, Handbook of the Global Trade Community*, 6th edition, World Trade Press, p. 117, 2005.
2. 46 CFR §515.2(m).
3. Hinkelman, Edward, *Dictionary of International Trade, Handbook of the Global Trade Community*, 6th edition, World Trade Press, 2005.
4. Ibid.
5. Ibid.
6. Ibid.
7. *Black's Law Dictionary*, 7th edition, West Group, p. 677, 1999.
8. 46 CFR §515.2(k).
9. 46 CFR §515.2(t).
10. *Black's Law Dictionary*, 7th edition, West Group, p. 159, 1999.
11. 46 USC §§1300–1315.
12. 46 USC §1300 *et. seq.*
13. Hinkelman, Edward, *Dictionary of International Trade, Handbook of the Global Trade Community*, 6th edition, World Trade Press, p. 46, 2005.
14. *International Chamber of Commerce Guide to Incoterms*, Jan Ramberg, ©International Chamber of Commerce (ICC), 2011.
15. US Customs ruling, HQ H079697, October 26, 2009.

Chapter 9

Incorporating sustainable fashion principles

Whether measured in terms of environmental impact, community building, or taken more literally to mean the protection and preservation of the industry itself, the recognition of the importance of sustainability is undeniably a regular part of today's business of fashion conversation.

Learning objectives

- Expand your understanding of sustainable fashion principles
- Attain practical advice for incorporating ethical business practices into your company's operations
- Design your own ethical code of conduct for outsourced labor

From luxury to everyday necessities, the design, production, sales, and transportation of fashion merchandise creates employment for hundreds of thousands of people, if not millions, worldwide. When you dig a little deeper, it becomes apparent that job creation derived from this industry extends to

- Farmers and shepherds;
- Factory workers (from fabrics, to packaging, to garment manufacturing, etc.);
- Air, vessel, truck, and rail transport and logistics providers;
- Marine terminals and warehousemen;
- Salespersons (both wholesale and retail);
- Corporate executives;
- Jobbers and distributors;
- Journalists, bloggers and book publishers;

- Universities, trade schools, and online instructors;
- Marketers and advertising companies;
- Information technology and web providers; and
- Several other direct and indirect product and service providers.

Given the reach the industry has on global employment, it naturally follows that implementing mechanisms to not merely sustain the industry but enable it to thrive, becomes imperative. While challenges and opportunities exist when it comes to sustainability, as shown by the momentum behind the concept of sustainability throughout the industry, the incorporation of sustainable practices is no longer a question of *if* they will be implemented, but *when* and *how*.

Which comes first: Business or vision?

You may be someone who has always loved clothes, someone in the business of selling them, or both. Either way, while the marriage of the ideology of "sustainable fashion" and "business operations" may be simple enough to comprehend, in practice there can be several challenges where business practices incorporating sustainable principles have not been thought through and planned for in advance of implementation.

As for which comes first, you need to have an actual revenue-generating business upon which your vision may be assessed against. Without one, there are no sustainable practices to implement. Therefore, if you are someone reading this who is contemplating starting a business that you can proudly declare is engaged in sustainable fashion, my recommendation would be to launch it with as many sustainable and ethical practices as can be supported at the outset. If you are reading this chapter from the perspective of someone who is already in business, think about your existing obligations and priorities to identify where the phasing in of sustainable practices may begin.

Shaping the vision for a different tomorrow

Protecting an industry—from itself in this case—requires not only specific actions but also the transformation of the collective thinking around it. We are seeing such shifting of the minds through the publication of books on sustainable fashion and living, such as *MAGNIFECO Your Head-to-Toe Guide to Ethical*

Fashion and Non-Toxic Beauty by author Kate Black[1], and *Zero Waste Fashion Design* by authors Timo Rissanen and Holly McQuillan.[2] There has also been a rise in university held events such as at Glasgow Caledonia's "Fair Fashion Center," and at the Fashion Institute of Technology (FIT), both institutions which have hosted events on sustainability, including those by Kate Black and her Eco-Sessions® series. We further see a shift in the terms used to describe emerging practices along with new terminology altogether, like the term "upcycling."

Upcycling

In the context of fashion, **upcycling**, as explained by Amy Du Fault, Director of Communications at Pratt University's Brooklyn Fashion + Design Accelerator (BF+DA) and sustainable fashion writer and consultant, is a process where post-consumer textiles are made into new apparel or accessories. According to Amy, "New York City residents throw away approximately 200,000 tons of clothing, shoes, handbags, belts, and other textiles and apparel annually. US households now generate an average of 82 pounds of textile waste per year."[3] Given these statistics, not only is an increase in upcycling needed, but changes in the way we think about secondhand goods and **repurposing** them, i.e., using goods that would otherwise be discarded towards another useful purpose, is needed. Thanks to the fast food, fast fashion, and other faster-is-better marketing messages pervading our society, the collective thinking of quickly using something and moving on to the next new thing has tainted what had formerly been popular paradigms of "built to last." Fortunately, today we are seeing a convergence of influences, including universities, leading companies, influential individuals, and technologies that are deepening the impact of sustainability and transforming it from a mere concept to actual conduct.

The evolution of the notion of "sustainable fashion"

While the benefits of having an accessible and immediate online dialogue about sustainable fashion cannot be overstated, having a structured setting for teaching those going into the industry is likewise needed for the expansion of this paradigm. Not only have institutions like FIT increased curricula, symposia, and other campus events on the subject of sustainable fashion, but we are seeing it globally as well, such as at the London College of Fashion.

Sustainable practices and attitudes towards fashion

I first met Professor Frances Corner OBE, Head of the London College of Fashion and Pro Vice-Chancellor of the University of the Arts London, while in India at a fashion conference where I spoke on sustainable fashion from a community building perspective in relation to the African fashion industry. Professor Corner in turn, spoke on sustainable practices and attitudes. In the Q&A with her presented in Box 9.1, Professor Corner shares how she sees the evolution of sustainable fashion and highlights a rise in consumer awareness and innovation through upcycling.

Box 9.1 Q&A: Professor Frances Corner on the evolution of the notion of sustainable fashion

Compared to two or three years ago how have you seen the notion of "sustainable fashion" evolve into what is today a regular part of the fashion industry's conversation?

In May 2007, *Vogue*® stated that sustainable fashion appeared not to be a short-term trend but one which could last multiple seasons. Three years ago I published my book, *Why Fashion Matters* which I wrote with the aim of inspiring changes in attitudes towards fashion, and it's potential as a vehicle for social change by inspiring sustainable consumer behavior. I found through my research that, today, sustainability is integral to the future success of the fashion industry and cannot be ignored.

Fashion has been around for a long time, and in many ways has sustained itself throughout the centuries. Fashion is a multi-billion pound industry providing tens of thousands of jobs and makes a significant contribution to the UK and global economy. Today, there is a need to create a system which can be supported in terms of environmentalism and social responsibility. In recent years there have been more sobering exposés of the reality behind high street fashion and its environmental and social impacts. From Uzbekistan cotton and its links with child labor, to animal farming and the consequences of western clothes shipped to Africa. Issues raised in recent years are becoming increasingly relevant. Designers are asking themselves what their clothing label might say if it had to inform the consumer of how it was made, a question which became especially pertinent in light of the Rana Plaza factory collapse in Bangladesh, which killed 1,129 people.

Retailers and designers are now starting to take a more positive look at alternative business models, and integrating sustainable practices into production, visiting factories in Bangladesh and China and exploring different materials, re-using old garments and upcycling.

Upcycling is now a huge part of the development of sustainable fashion. Today more designers are working with recycled materials and discarded garments than ever before. This way of producing encourages innovation by making use of all manner of materials, from human hair, linen sheets, flour bags, and military tents.

Consumers today are more aware of the cost of cheap fashion, and are voting with their feet. There are many facets to the challenge however; it's not all about supply chain and production. The UK throws out 350,000 tons of clothes into landfill every year. Sustainable fashion isn't just about having something eco-friendly, it's also about considering the use, value and disposal of our garments. There are now a whole host of sustainability initiatives like textile recycling and fair trade schemes from brands including People Tree®, M&S®, and Timberland®.

Supply chain, production, and disposal are huge challenges, but today there are many other considerations which are only just beginning to come to the fore; from branding and identity, ethical leadership and collaborative ways of working, making use of technologies as well as communication and harnessing the power of social media, to considering the social impact of our work as designers, retailers, and consumers.

The emergence of the sustainable and ethical fashion business

More than that of other behemoth industries, including that of automobiles and electronics, the fashion industry's enlightenment around social issues has seen a recent evolution that is gaining momentum and proving to be more than just a passing trend. While the concept of sustainable and ethical fashion have been notably growing subjects of interest for the fashion industry over the last five to eight years, uncertainty has arisen in relation to what these terms actually mean. Ultimately, the way this is defined will depend on the person answering the question and based on their definition, it will shape how such considerations get incorporated into either an existing business, or how they will be implemented from scratch.

Sustainable and ethical considerations

While priorities may vary, sustainable and ethical considerations for the fashion industry include:

- The health and well-being of workers, whether physical mental, or emotional.
- Environmental concerns, including minimizing pollutants, reducing energy use, or otherwise.
- Fair wages and their appropriateness for an acceptable standard of living (as measured within a worker's own country).
- The integrity of the inputs used to make the raw materials that merchandise is made out of (e.g., non-toxic materials, organic fibers).
- Sourcing transparency and supply chain integrity.

These considerations may be applied to the internal practices a company implements, to third parties from whom services are outsourced, such as garment manufacturing, or both.

Adopting a broader approach to ethical and sustainable fashion issues

Adopting a broader approach to ethical and sustainable fashion issues extends beyond that of accounting for the quality-of-life issues surrounding garment or other workers laboring under typical factory conditions. Concerns include those of both obvious and less obvious participants impacted directly and indirectly by the industry. An obvious example of a directly impacted participant is that of models and the amount of food they are able to consume while remaining an "attractive" candidate for a modeling job, or their fair compensation for being photographed. An example of an indirectly impacted participant is that of the children of laborers whose low wages are insufficient for covering the cost of their school fees, and therefore leave the children uneducated. Given the variation and breadth of considerations a company's unique footprint may give rise to, when considering in which areas to implement sustainable practices, the importance of taking the time for advance thought and planning on this subject, even if only minimal, cannot be overstated.

Drafting a meaningful mission statement

From *Forbes*® and *Entrepreneur*® magazine, to several other publications in both hardcopy and electronic form, there is no shortage of advice on how to write a mission statement. The traditional method of formulating one revolves around defining what a company is about and why it exists. It may also include a company's objectives for fulfilling its mission with statements being centered around the customer satisfaction attained from the "value" a product or service offers its consumers. In the context of sustainable and ethical fashion however, this statement would include an added dimension to account for such objectives that a company's leadership seeks to address.

Incorporating sustainable and ethical considerations into your business model

Common questions asked when deciding on how to implement sustainable and ethical considerations into a business include:

1 How can I create business practices that incorporate the principles which have the most meaning to me?

2 Do I attempt to implement all of these principles at once, or should they be phased in once specific milestones have been reached?

3 Would it make more sense to prioritize my list of what I want to achieve and start with what is currently viable for the business?

As stated earlier in this chapter, it is critical to have an operational business generating revenue. Therefore, in relation to this last question, as should be done with all business decisions, prioritizing what can be done within a particular timeframe and budget is an evaluation to be made when incorporating ethical and sustainable practices. Given the necessity of purchasing goods and services to run a business, a natural starting place for implementing such practices is that of sourcing.

How can I engage in ethical sourcing?

There are thousands of manufacturers from whom goods may be sourced from around the globe. Given the variances on product availability, quality, expediency, transportation costs, and other factors, irrespective of where you choose to source from, by having your own set of ethical sourcing guidelines you can ensure that purchasing decisions are made from a place of mindfulness in relation to your company's ethics.

The United Nations (UN) describes **supply chain sustainability** as the "management of environmental, social and economic impacts and the encouragement of good governance practices, throughout the lifecycles of goods and services." [4] With so much fashion merchandise being manufactured overseas, it follows that maintaining a baseline of accountability for the basic human rights of foreign laborers is an area increasingly gaining importance in the industry. As such, when working with manufacturers it is not uncommon for a brand to have its suppliers agree to certain terms in relation to employee treatment and working conditions, as shown in Box 9.2. Not only is an agreement to abide by the terms sought, but an extension of such terms could also regulate (attempt to anyway) such third party vendors from whom the manufacturer itself might hire.

Box 9.2 Clauses for creating an ethical code of conduct for outsourced labor

Here are ten sample contract provisions which can be used as a basis for creating a company's own ethical sourcing code of conduct.[5]

Code of Conduct: Legal and Ethical Business Practices of Suppliers

Child labor: You and your suppliers will not purchase products or components manufactured by persons younger than fifteen (15) years of age, or younger than the age of completing compulsory education in the country of manufacture, where such age is higher than fifteen (15). You and your suppliers further acknowledge and agree that in no case shall any child younger than fifteen (15) years of age, or younger than the age of completing compulsory education in the country of manufacture where such age is higher than fifteen (15), be employed in the manufacturing, packaging, sales, or distribution of merchandise.

Forced labor: You and your suppliers will not purchase products or components from suppliers that use forced labor, prison labor, indentured labor, or exploited bonded labor, or permit their suppliers to do so. You and your suppliers acknowledge and agree that you will only employ persons whose presence is voluntary and that they will not utilize any forced or involuntary labor, whether prison, bonded, indentured or otherwise.

Contract labor: You and your suppliers shall not use workers obligated under contracts which exploit them, deny them the basic legal rights available to people and to workers within the countries in which they work, or which are inconsistent with the principles set forth in this *Code of Conduct: Legal and Ethical Business Practices of Suppliers*. You and your suppliers must fully comply with all applicable local, state, federal, national and international laws, rules and regulations including, but not limited to, those relating to wages, hours, labor, health and safety, and immigration.

Work hours: You and your suppliers shall not require employees to work more than the limits on regular and overtime hours allowed by the law of the country of manufacture. Except under extraordinary business circumstances, you and your suppliers' employees shall be entitled to at least one (1) day off in every seven (7) day period. You and your suppliers must inform workers at the time of hiring if mandatory overtime is a condition of their employment and shall not compel them to work excessive overtime hours.

Wages and benefits: You and your suppliers recognize that wages are essential to meeting employees' basic needs and shall pay employees at least the minimum wage required by local law regardless of whether they are paid by the piece or by the hour, and shall provide legally mandated benefits.

Overtime compensation: Your and your suppliers' employees shall be compensated for overtime hours at such premium rate as is legally required in the country of manufacture or, in countries where such laws do not exist, at a rate at least equal to their regular hourly compensation rate.

Freedom of association: You and your suppliers shall recognize and respect the right of employees to freely associate in accordance with the laws of the countries in which they are employed.

Nondiscrimination: You and your suppliers shall not subject any person to discrimination in employment, including hiring, salary, benefits, advancement, discipline, termination or retirement, on the basis of gender, race, religion, age, disability, sexual orientation, nationality, political opinion, or social or ethnic origin.

Harassment or abuse: You and your suppliers must treat employees with respect and dignity. No employee shall be subject to physical, sexual or psychological harassment or abuse. You and your suppliers acknowledge and agree not to use corporal punishment or threats of violence.

Health and safety: You and your suppliers shall provide a safe and healthy working environment to prevent accidents and injury to health arising out of, linked with, or occurring in the course of work, or as a result of the operation of employer facilities. You and your suppliers further acknowledge and agree that you will comply with all applicable workplace conditions, safety and environmental laws.

When working with an attorney on a contract governing vendor relationships, a company may consider how these provisions, or a version similar to these, may be drafted either into the contract itself, or as an attachment incorporated by reference. At the very least, a willingness to agree to such language would enable a company to identify which vendors are amenable to the terms versus those who are not, which may make the decision on which supplier to use an easier one.

Considerations toward sustainable design

Approaching the incorporation of sustainable and ethical practices into a business can be a daunting process. As shared by Timo Rissanen PhD, Assistant Professor of Fashion Design and Sustainability, Parsons The New School for Design (Box 9.3), having a long term approach to continuously learn more about sustainability is a way forward in and of itself.

Box 9.3 Q&A: Timo Rissanen, PhD on approaching sustainability

What's an efficient way to think about and discuss sustainability?

There are no quick and easy solutions to sustainability. Sustainability in fashion is complex and messy, and it is easy to use that as an excuse not to think about it. The complexity and messiness must be acknowledged. The good news is that nobody can be an expert on every aspect of sustainability in fashion; it is simply too complex and vast. Much good information is available freely, and start-ups that have a genuine interest in sustainability (one that is not merely a marketing tactic) tend to support each other around the various issues. For example, I've witnessed small companies joining forces to order the same fabric in order to meet the fabric mill's minimum. In the old fashion paradigm of secrecy and paranoia, that would have been unheard of.

My suggestion to a start-up would be to approach sustainability as a never-ending learning experience. There is no place to get to; rather, I'd encourage a company to continuously learn more and act accordingly over time. One of the many advantages start-ups have over existing brands, particularly large ones, is that they can build sustainability into the core values of the business. In the face of tightening regulations and increasing consumer demand for transparency and compliance, this is a real advantage.

Reality bites—challenges to running a "sustainable" business

Easing your way into incorporating sustainable practices has been emphasized in this chapter due to the burnout that can occur when attempting to incorporate too many at once without any flexibility to cease or modify their application. As shared by design and production process consultant Anthony Lilore (Box 9.4), who is notably a founding board member of NYC's Save the Garment Center, and a designer at RESTORE Clothing, it is necessary to have a viable business that is operating profitably in order for it to successfully exist while maintaining its sustainable agenda.

Box 9.4 Q&A: Incorporating sustainable principles into the ethical enterprise, an interview with Anthony Lilore, Designer at RESTORE Clothing

1. Describe some of the challenges RESTORE Clothing ran into in operating a "sustainable" business and lessons learned from self-imposed restrictions that, as you have described, left the business too narrowly defined to operate.

The challenges that RESTORE Clothing ran into in operating a sustainable business are the same challenges most companies, clothing or otherwise, run into in trying to operate a business. First and foremost the definition of sustainable was internally misinterpreted to have meant "Green and Eco", as opposed to self-perpetuating. Too much energy, effort and concentration was spent sticking to the clearly defined and self imposed restrictions associated with the acronym RESTORE: Responsible, Earth friendly, Sustainable, Technological, Organic, Recycled, Ergonomic. Such constraints work for Opera and Sonnets, however this acronym, while gallant and apparently clearly defined, actually clouded our view and improperly focused our mission. Again the misinterpretation of Sustainable was an error.

2. What are your top five considerations that you would recommend be kept in mind when starting a business?

The top five considerations that I would recommend are as follows:

(a) Does your company have a reason to be? Is there a point of difference that your company brings to the market that separates you and your product from the existing offering by your competitors? Truly this means, "do you have a reason to exist?" A t-shirt with three sleeves does not have a reason to exist just because nobody else in the market is doing it. Does a market exist for your product? Can you make it and sell it at a profit? Can you scale it, and do it better than the company that is going to knock you off?

(b) Can you afford to be in business? Can you afford success? Can you afford a failure and a re-launch in order to remain sustainable? Remember sustainability does not mean just Green and Eco, can you afford the dollars required to stay in business?

(c) Do you have the right partners? Are you part of a group that is made up of co-dependent areas of expertise?

(d) Are you fully aware of the market you are planning to enter? Do you know who the competition is and how they are succeeding within the space?

(e) Do you have a passion to do this, i.e., to enter into a marketplace with your product even in the face of great adversity? Do you have the passion to sustain your business? Can you account for every detail in the cost of bringing your product to market? Do you know and understand business math? Can you be objective? Do you know the difference between optimism and realism?

3. In the context of running a social good business, if a company is looking to have a "moral conscience," discuss the importance of having a business perspective that celebrates meeting one or two of the social good outcomes the company hopes to meet with the aim to accomplish the others in the future.

The refusal to except *very good* in lieu of *perfect* was an error (re-read point 1). In the case of RESTORE, achieving one or two of the acronym parameters while striving for more later would have been a smarter path. In the context of running a socially conscious business, ask whether you have the perspective to do good or to do better. Not, "better than the next guy," but better then yourself yesterday. In short, it is admirable to have a moral compass and moral goals, but that is a sliding scale based on incremental achievements. Strive to do your moral best by being morally better today than yesterday and better still tomorrow. (Now, re-read points 1 and 2).

"Scaling in" sustainable practices into your business

In the spirit of accepting *very good* in lieu of *perfect*, we can now examine how sustainable and ethical practices may be scaled into a new or existing business. Professor Corner from the London College of Fashion shares her top five areas for consideration when embarking on doing so (Box 9.5).

Box 9.5 Q&A: Professor Frances Corner on incorporating sustainable fashion principles into business operations

What are your top five considerations that you would recommend to a company seeking to incorporate sustainable fashion principles into their operations?

1 Consider your resources and materials. Are they ethically and sustainably sourced? Are they recycled, upcycled and recyclable? You might want to consider sourcing materials and other resources sustainably, perhaps from local suppliers.

2 Consider your supply chain, and production methods. What are the working conditions like for the people manufacturing your garments? It's not just about the carbon footprint of your creations; it's also about considering the social and economic impacts of your business.

3 Net positive strategies are built on the idea that a company must give back more than it takes from society and the environment. Consider the social impact of your work and you may even want to consider pioneering a net positive strategy.

4 Consider your brand identity and where your sustainable practice fits into this. Not everyone wants to market their brand as "sustainable fashion," but be sure to tell your sustainability stories. Sustainable practice can be incorporated into anything from production (by making use of new materials and technologies), communication (by harnessing the power of social media) to leadership and ways of working.

5 Consider how you run your company. Ethical leadership can have significant influence, not only on your employees, but also the people you work with and sell to. By incorporating collaborative ways of working into your business practice, a start-up can obtain better access to knowledge, resources, also recognition and reward, when facing competition for finite resources.

When customer opinion shapes business decisions

With the ubiquity of computers, laptops, cell phones, tablets, and wireless capabilities, consumers have quick access to not just the retailers they buy from, but also to industry production methods, information on a company's environmental impact, and several other issues. Consumers are also asking what "social good" can be done by the retailers to whom their consumer dollars support, and the answer affects not only the choices shoppers make about the brands and retailers they buy from, but how much they spend with them.

Connecting consumers to the brand—incorporating sustainable practices into the retail story

A **conscious consumer** is one who makes purchasing decisions based on factors that extend beyond the mere aesthetic or functionality of the article, which can include a company's business practices. Such decision making could occur due to a negative incident that shines a spotlight on the poor governance of a corporation, or it could arise from a company's own marketing of its positive social agenda, such as that of outdoor clothing retailer Patagonia, Inc. The company has taken a 360-degree look at its business and today publishes an annual report on its social and environmental initiatives.

Patagonia as a leading example

From tracing the feathers in its down jackets and creating a standard upon which others can adopt in relation to manufacturing with feathers,[6] to paying their employees to volunteer for two months with an environmental group of their choice, to its responsible sourcing approach,[7] Patagonia is not only at the forefront of what it means to be a sustainable and ethical fashion business, but the accompanying social good story consumers are listening to makes shoppers feel good about the pricey merchandise they are purchasing. The example Patagonia is setting is a great starting place for exposure to the possibilities of operating a sustainable company. Further details about the company itself and their several initiatives can be found at www.patagonia.com, and all businesses should be encouraged to gain insight and inspiration from Patagonia when outlining considerations for their own sustainable design.

Resources for more information

The United Nations Global Compact encourages companies to make sustainability a priority from the top of an organization. The following three publications are free resources to assist companies with meeting this challenge.

Supply Chain Sustainability – A Practical Guide for Continuous Improvement, Second Edition: https://www.unglobalcompact.org/library/205

A Guide to Traceability: A Practical Approach to Advance Sustainability in Global Supply Chains: https://www.unglobalcompact.org/library/791

Support your SME (Small and Medium-Sized) Supplier: https://www.unglobalcompact.org/docs/issues_doc/supply_chain/SMEsinSupplyChain.pdf

Key terms

conscious consumer	supply chain	upcycling
repurposing	sustainability	

Discussion questions and exercises

1 If you were incorporating socially responsible principles into your business, what top three (3) would you choose and why?

2 If you could choose only five (5) clauses for creating an ethical code of conduct for outsourced labor listed in Box 9.2, which would you choose? For each, explain why you selected this option.

3 Choose two of the clothing articles you are currently wearing. State what they are and how you would repurpose them into another product(s) for a different use.

4 Research online fashion magazines, blogs, or other periodicals to find a recent incident involving a garment manufacturer and a negative incident. Prepare a one- to two-page description of your plan for the company to avoid this situation arising again in the future.

Notes

1. Black, K. (2015), *MAGNIFECO Your Head-to-Toe Guide to Ethical Fashion and Non-Toxic Beauty*. Canada: New Society Publishers.
2. Rissanen, T., McQuillan, H. (2016), *Zero Waste Fashion Design*. New York: Bloomsbury Academic.
3. https://www.theguardian.com/sustainable-business/haiti-fashion-clothing-recycling-upcycling (viewed on February 9, 2017).

4. UN Global Compact Office and BSR (2015), *Supply Chain Sustainability, A Practical Guide for Continuous Improvement*, 2d Edition.

5. *See generally*, UN Supplier Code of Conduct, Rev. 04, January 2011.

6. www.patagonia.com/traceabledown (viewed on February 11, 2017).

7. www.patagonia.com/footprint (viewed on February 11, 2017).

Chapter 10

Emerging fashion industry issues

From online technologies and wearable ones, to fashion accelerators and incubators, the fashion industry is experiencing a renaissance in the products themselves, how business is getting done, the support systems for new designers and companies, and the way merchandise is now being sold. Where a business is pursuing an emerging area presented in this chapter or elsewhere, be it through the acquisition or consideration of funding opportunities (for which lawyers should be retained to analyze such agreements), to the manufacture of a wearable technology overseas, there are several ways a company could benefit from consultation with an attorney on both obvious and unforeseen legal implications. It is recommended that such guidance be obtained.

Learning objectives

- Discern the funding options available to a fashion business
- Understand what it means to establish a "benefit corporation"
- Differentiate between a fashion incubator and fashion accelerator
- Gain insight and strategies on how to manage a successful crowdfunding campaign

The emergence of "fashion tech" and wearable technology

The marriage between fashion and technology has led to the emergence of a new line of products dubbed as "fashion tech" or "wearable technology." While the fitness space led the way for the market expansion of these products, such as with the Fitbit®, other more cost prohibitive accessories such as Google Glass® (Figure 10.1), only enjoyed a short period of media hype prior to its steady decline. Products offering greater functionality, such as Apple, Inc.'s Apple Watch®, includes features such as telephone answering capabilities and photo viewing. It also has enjoyed a recognition by brands like Hermes®, who partnered with Apple, Inc., to add handcrafted leather bands and a Hermes® inscripted watch face to offer what they describe as "an elegant way to live a better day."[1]

Smart fabrics

As innovators continue to forge new roads into the wearable technology space, high-tech developments in fabrics have expanded the category of **smart fabrics**. These offer a specific functionality due to the incorporation of certain chemicals into the fabrics and result in, for example, increased fire retardation or water repellence.

Online technologies and fashion

A further expansion of the application of fashion technology is seen in the e-commerce arena, whether with respect to tools enhancing the consumer experience around sizing and fit capabilities, or with smart phone applications that can, for example, compare in-store to online pricing so that shoppers can obtain the best possible price on merchandise.

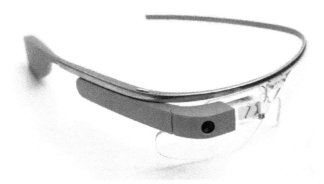

Figure 10.1 Google Glass® eyewear. Source: iStock/comferrantraite.

Fashion incubators and accelerators

Fashion incubators

The Merriam-Webster dictionary defines an **incubator** as "an organization or place that aids the development of new business ventures especially by providing low-cost commercial space, management assistance, or shared services."[2] In the context of fashion, an incubator is further designed to provide a nurturing environment for the budding fashion start-up. As shown in Box 10.1, there are several fashion incubators in major cities both in the US and abroad, and they share a common methodology for supporting their designers in residence.

Box 10.1 Incubators and accelerators[3]

US based

NY Fashion Tech Lab: http://www.nyftlab.com

Trendseeder: http://www.trendseeder.com/pages/trendseeder-accelerator

Fashion Incubator SF: www.fashionincubatorsf.org

Manufacture New York: http://manufactureny.org

Le French Lab (in Los angeles promoting French brands/designers): http://www.lefrenchlab.fr/about/

Seattle Fashion Incubator: seattlefashionincubator.org

Portland Apparel Lab: http://portlandapparellab.com

Philadelphia Fashion Incubator: http://www.philadelphiafashionincubator.com

Council of Fashion Designers of America (CFDA): http://cfda.com/programs/cfda-fashion-incubator

International

France—Maisons de Mode: http://www.maisonsdemode.com/en/presentation/

Dubai—Fashion Incubator: http://www.dubaifashionincubator.com/

Estonia—Incubator Tallinn: inkubaator.tallinn.ee/eng/

London—Front Row I/O: http://frontrowio.com/

Canada—Toronto Fashion Incubator: http://fashionincubator.on.ca/

Australia—Creative Enterprise Australia Incubator: http://qutcea.com/

Generally speaking, a fashion incubator provides resources to a small group of emerging apparel or accessories designers for a duration lasting between three months to one year. Resources can include a space to work (e.g., production and showroom space), mentoring, and a structured course curriculum.

Incubators with a specific focus

Some incubators focus on supporting a specific type of entrepreneur, such as the New York Fashion Tech Lab (NYFTL), which focuses on developing companies that have created "innovations at the center of fashion retail, and technology."[4] Others, like the Philadelphia Fashion Incubator (PFI), offer support to only locally based businesses whose merchandise is within the accessories or apparel categories. Thanks to the relationships an incubator has with key consultants, executives, retailers, and others within the fashion industry, some of whom serve as mentors to those participating in the program, designers obtain not merely a unique curriculum for advancing their business, but also an opportunity to connect with industry leaders who can provide exposure to people and resources which may not have otherwise been accessible.

The spotlight shines on graduates

A final fashion show, as is done at the Macys City Center location in Philadelphia for PFI residents, provides participants with an opportunity to showcase their merchandise, as does the graduation event for the NYFTL, wherein other fashion industry insiders, innovators, investors, and retailers are invited to meet the designers and, of course, discuss purchasing and investment opportunities. These events further attract the press whose media coverage provides additional opportunities for the brand's expanding recognition.

Fashion accelerators

The New York City based Pratt Institute has its Brooklyn Fashion and Design Accelerator (BF+DA) dedicated to supporting entrepreneurs in building successful businesses that integrate the environment and society into their bottom line. Designers can explore the intersection of fashion and technology and they have access to state of the art 3D printers and a lab for textile innovation, knitting machines as shown in Figure 10.2, and laser cutters.

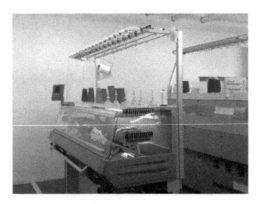

Figure 10.2 Knitting machine at BF+DA Source: Deanna Clark-Esposito.

It is not uncommon to hear the term "fashion incubator" and "fashion accelerator" used interchangeably, however there are differences. As described more fully in Box 10.2 by Amy Du Fault, the Director of Communications at BF+DA and a sustainable fashion writer and consultant, an incubator can be thought of as a foundation for a bigger house, whereas an accelerator is a space for taking the already constructed foundation and building upon it. Irrespective of the accelerator or incubator chosen, each present a tremendous opportunity to the early stage startup to successfully launch and grow a viable business.

Box 10.2 What is the difference between a fashion accelerator and fashion incubator? By Amy Du Fault

An incubator is a space to take fresh talent and let them percolate a little bit as to how they will run their business, if they have the backbone and the passion to take their business from beyond a startup to something more substantial. I think of it as a foundation for a bigger house.

An accelerator is a space for really taking the foundation and building. It's a space for considering what success is now that one has a glimmer of it. It's a place for mentorship, tough love and all the tools for accelerating the speed of a business—then running with it. It's where you get your doctorate, your "second floor of the house," and all through the use of an active community that urges you on that you can do it!!!!

Preparing the application

Once an entrepreneur has identified an incubator or accelerator that fits its particular focus, the question of "does my business meet the minimum requirements to apply?" becomes an issue. Providers typically require that an applicant has been in business for a minimum amount of time and has already had sales in the marketplace. A demonstrable commitment by the entrepreneur to dedicate its time to the business that would be equivalent to a full-time job is sought, together with a major commitment to build and sustain the budding enterprise. Reasons such as an inability to attend all courses or to come in and work at the dedicated space can be the basis for ineligibility for acceptance. In addition, some programs have a mandatory application fee along with an ongoing monthly fee for the duration of the program which must be paid.

Financing and funding the fashion business

When entering the fashion industry, business owners may combine the resources they have using personal savings, gifts, or loans from friends and family. While credit cards may also be used, this type of financing can get expensive fast due to the high interest rates that accompany a credit card. In addition to this, it simply does not under most circumstances provide enough capital to actually fund the operations of a business.

Traditional methods of finance

A business loan from a bank is a traditional method of financing a business and is typically sought out by business owners. Provided the company has a good credit history, this will not be a problem to obtain and it would have the freedom to use the money as it deemed fit. Where a business has either not been in existence long enough to establish a credit history, or its owners have a less than desirable credit history such that a bank would not want to lend money to the applicant, there are resources such as the US Small Business Administration (SBA) which has several different loan options available.

The SBA loan framework

While the SBA is not a bank itself, it does provide a guarantee to the actual bank lending the money. That is, by obtaining a loan via an SBA program, in the event the borrower does not repay the loan, i.e. **defaults** on the loan, the SBA having guaranteed the loan, would ultimately reimburse the bank for its loss. Be advised that money obtained through an SBA loan may have certain spending limitations attached to it. A company may, for example, be required to spend it only on purchases such as to acquire machinery or equipment, to renovate the building which the business will occupy, or to use it to finance existing business debt.[5]

SBA loan options

The SBA has several loan options available depending on the type of business seeking a loan. For example, if a business owner is considering manufacturing apparel in the US and wants to sell overseas, there are loans specifically designated for exporters which can be applied for. These will likely increase in popularity as more cities dedicate financing to new apparel manufacturing hubs, as New York City's Mayor Bill Di Blasio announced in February 2017 in Sunset Park, Brooklyn.[6] More information, including the maximum loan amounts and minimum requirements for applicants of an SBA loan, can be found on the SBA website at www.sba.gov.

Crowdfunding the fashion venture

Where traditional lending is not available or of interest to a company, embarking on a **crowdfunding** campaign, that is sourcing funds through several people who do not have to be repaid, is a popular option. Crowdfunding is typically used to finance a specific short term project that a business seeks to accomplish. Created and executed through an online platform, several of which are shown in Figure 10.3, they provide a means for businesses to both promote their mission while raising capital.

Figure 10.3 Various online crowdfunding platforms. Source: iStock.com/bonetta.

While crowdfunding is a way to raise money for all types of ventures and projects, in terms of fashion it is often used for production costs, the revamping or expansion of a website, or to fund a fashion show. While there are several crowdfunding platforms to consider, as listed in Box 10.3, one popular platform for crowdfunding in the fashion industry is Kickstarter whose mission is to "help bring creative projects to life."[7]

Kickstarter

Formed in 2009, it has had over ten million people back a Kickstarter campaign across all projects worldwide.[9] Its rules require that there be a clear goal and dollar amount for the funding of a specific activity whereby the proceeds raised during the Kickstarter campaign will be used towards an effort that will be completed.[10] Money supporting a project is known as a **pledge**, which is a sum of money guaranteed for payment in the event the stated dollar goal for the campaign has been reached. This, in fact, is an important caveat to note of a crowdfunding campaign, as where the overall campaign total is not reached, those who made a pledge during the campaign are not obligated to pay. That is, where the aggregate of all money pledged does not meet the funding goal, for example only $4,500 is raised during a campaign seeking to raise $5,000, the project itself is not funded.[11] In such an event, those running the campaign may elect to correspond individually with those who made a pledge and request they contribute anyway despite not having reached the goal. Depending on the project and the relationship between the donor and the campaigner, they may opt to support the campaign anyway, so it is worth asking the question where the funding goal has not been reached.

Box 10.3 Crowdfunding platforms[8]

- I AM LAMODE: http://www.iamlamode.com/en
- Indiegogo: https://www.indiegogo.com/choose-your-platform
- Kickstarter: https://www.kickstarter.com
- Rocket Hub: https://www.rockethub.com/funding

Preparing for a successful campaign

Positioning a company for a successful crowdfunding campaign begins with preparing for the execution of each phase of it. Shanley Knox, co-founder of sustainable accessories brand, Olivia Knox, raised money using the crowdfunding platform Indiegogo for the funding of a project to support manufacturing capabilities in Uganda for her jewelry company. As described in Box 10.4, she lends her advice on how to construct and run a successful campaign.

Box 10.4 Q&A with Shanley Knox, co-founder of Olivia Knox: Advice for having a successful crowdfunding campaign

1. Please describe the strategy of your crowdfunding campaign, why you chose the platform you did, and what you believe made it a success.

My crowdfunding campaign was a collaborative effort between myself and a friend in New York who developed the video for the campaign. The goal was to raise funding to launch our cooperation, pay legal fees, audit a facility in Uganda and really get us off the ground, in general. Before launching, I reached out to both my existing network and people I saw were social media influencers within networks I believed would be interested in my work. This group of people, together, agreed to help my cause by sending out social media posts to spread awareness. Throughout the campaign, I sent out emails that touched in different, sensitive areas of our work. For instance: my dreams as a young female entrepreneur, the ways in which we want to integrate women into our business, and the potential to shift an economy in Uganda.

I believe it was successful because of careful planning and strategy, building up an existing network and the way we used content to touch on different areas so as to involve the priorities and passions of many different types of people.

We used Indiegogo because it is instant, the fees are low, and it's quite easy to build out your own campaign.

2. Every campaign includes a description of who the business is and what it's aiming to achieve. What was yours?

Olivia Knox is a manufacturing company based in Uganda and New York City. We exclusively work with Ankole horn—the most diversely colored, dense and sizable horn in the world. Through this work, we are committed to "changing the face of manufacturing" through developing a reliable supply chain for luxury markets, while incorporating ethical practices, world class training programs, and competitive positions for men and women, equally.

3. What advice would you give other fashion brands?

I believe everything begins and ends with relationship. When you walk into a coffee meeting, you should be listening to your gut and noticing if the person you are meeting with is someone you know you want to have a relationship with for the long term. If so, it does not matter if they are buying a product, offering a service or throwing out a deal immediately. It matters that you become someone who knows them—that you take interest in their work, and update them on yours. Someday, it may be useful for you to know them. In the meantime, seek to care about them as a person on a journey that is intersecting with yours. Give when you can. Take when you can. This strategy of being true and having integrity and showing your real self to others within the fashion world has never led me astray. Instead, its kept me from petty conflicts, provided me with an incredibly valuable network, and provided a support system for myself as a young female entrepreneur.

Keep this kind of commitment in mind throughout all your communication, whether online or in real life. When people contribute, make sure you thank them so as to drive followers to their account. Be respectful. Think of ways to give back to them in a way that actually provides value for them, rather than simply showing yourself as someone that has a good amount of followers. It is always, always about building a two-way street.

Lastly, study good social media strategy, and implement it as much as possible. If necessary, hire someone on a one time contract to help run your campaign for you. My background happens to be in journalism and content marketing, so that proved very helpful for me in this regard.

4. What do you wish you had known before the campaign and how would you have done things differently, if at all?

I wish I had known how many people were interested in supporting me. In my career as a young, female entrepreneur, particularly one within the fashion world, I've often been afraid to put myself out there, to ask for advice, for one more donation, to admit my failures to those that have supported me. This campaign showed me how many people were still there behind me, believing in me and investing, not just in my business, but in myself as a person. That's really, really key—people invest in you. People communicate with you. Your business will never gain support if people don't believe in you as an individual. I was thrilled, and humbled, to see how many people still believed in me.

Traditional corporate forms and the new "benefit corporation"

While forming a corporate structure is not an emerging fashion industry issue, opting to establish what is known as a "benefit corporation" is. Prior to exploring this concept however, a general overview about corporate entities is warranted.

New businesses opt to take on a corporate form for reasons including to protect the owner's assets against financial and other liabilities, or to position itself to have investors whereby shares of stock representing a certain percentage of a company may be exchanged for capital. A US corporation is most commonly formed by the filing of a certificate of incorporation with the Department of State office within the state the business is physically located in, i.e., is a **resident** of. Each state has its own corporate filing process and fee structure for the payment of forming the business entity. As corporations are governed by state law, each state has its own legal formalities regarding the creation and ongoing obligations for operating a corporation, such as requirements for **shareholders**, i.e., the owners of a corporation, to meet annually to elect or re-elect members to its Board of Directors, to conduct meetings to make critical business decisions, and to memorialize such meetings by note taking in what are known as **minutes**. In addition, the creation of a corporation triggers tax reporting and payment obligations, and the types of taxes a corporation is liable for turns on whether the company has elected for tax treatment as an "S-Corp" or to remain subject to the tax scheme it obtains upon the formation of the corporation, which is being taxed under Subchapter C of the US tax code.

The S-Corporation

An **S-Corp**, i.e., a corporation eligible for tax treatment under Subchapter S of the US tax code, qualifies for this election where all of the shareholders agree to such designation and there are no more than 100 resident shareholders in the entity. In addition, there can only be one class of stock that has been issued, and all of the shareholders must either be individuals or estates, and not other companies. The primary reason for making an S-Corp election is for the owners to avoid being taxed twice, that is, being required to pay taxes on (1) the corporate earnings and then again, on (2) the shareholder's income, whose salaries or other distributions are paid by the corporation. Under the S-Corp election, the US Internal Revenue Service (IRS) allows for the corporation's profits and losses to pass through to the personal income taxes of the shareholders.

Another benefit of having an S-Corp is that in terms of liabilities, they are absorbed by the corporation instead of extending to a shareholder's own personal assets. These remain protected and shielded against corporate liabilities as long as it and its shareholders abide by the laws that govern corporations, including maintaining the finances of the corporation separate from those of the shareholders. In practice, this means that the shareholders would refrain from spending corporate funds for personal use.

The C-Corporation

Where a company opts not to elect for S-Corp status with the IRS, it maintains the tax treatment status it obtained at the time of incorporation which is taxation under Subchapter C of the US tax code. For this reason, the company is referred to as a **C-Corp**. While double taxation will occur, i.e. taxing both the corporation and its shareholders separately, a C-Corp is preferred where stocks have been or will be issued in different classes to accommodate sales of shares to investors. For this reason, where a company anticipates seeking investors, this corporate form will often be chosen.

Limited liability corporation

A limited liability corporation, otherwise known as an LLC, is a popular choice of business entity due to the protection it affords the owners. Technically called **members**, the owners can maintain an LLC without all of the formalities and paperwork required by a corporation. An LLC can have an unlimited number of members and is free to choose its management at the members' discretion. It can be comprised of either several individuals, various existing business entities, or any combination of individuals and existing business entities, none of whom are required to be citizens of the US. There is also the possibility for the formation of a **sole proprietor LLC**, which is an LLC comprised of only one member. This form is attractive to small business owners who want to avoid the double taxation requirement of a C-Corp and the corporate formalities of an S-Corp.

An LLC is formed by filing its Articles of Organization with a state's Department of State office. While state requirements can vary, once the formation has occurred, some states, such as New York, have a publication requirement where an LLC must announce that it has been created, through the publishing of a statement regarding its formation, in two local newspapers within 120 days of formation. Due to the high cost involved in publishing in a local newspaper in an expensive city like New York, where a company's resources are limited, it may elect to choose a different corporate form.

An **operating agreement** is required to establish how the LLC will operate. It can include information such as how profits and losses will be shared and how many members it will have. An LLC is authorized to hold real estate and personal property, and remains in existence until either the last remaining member of it dissolves the LLC, or the terms in the operating agreement provide for the occurrence of when the LLC would automatically cease to operate.

The benefit corporation

The laws governing the corporate form have been amended in several, but not all, states in America to provide the option for a company to incorporate as a "benefit corporation." A **benefit corporation** is that which is obligated to not only comply with the corporate requirements set forth for the corporate entity types described above, but in addition to this, is further formed for the purpose of creating a general public benefit.[12] A **general public benefit** is a "material positive impact on society and the environment, taken as a whole, assessed against a third party standard, from the business operations of [the] benefit corporation."[13]

As an example, in New York State a benefit corporation in its certificate of incorporation must state that "the corporation is a benefit corporation under Article 17 of the Business Corporation Law."[14] It may also include a statement of one or more "specific public benefit" purposes as listed in Box 10.5.

The rise of certification organizations

As explained above, one of the requirements to be a benefit corporation is having an independent third party assess the "benefit" being conferred by the corporation. One certification organization that was integral to the spearheading of legislative efforts to create the benefit corporation as a legal type of corporate

Box 10.5 Types of specific public benefits[15]

1 Providing low-income or underserved individuals or communities with beneficial products or services.

2 Promoting economic opportunity for individuals or communities beyond the creation of jobs in the normal course of business.

3 Preserving the environment.

4 Improving human health.

5 Promoting the arts, sciences or advancement of knowledge.

6 Increasing the flow of capital to entities with a public benefit purpose.

7 The accomplishment of any other particular benefit for society or the environment.

Box 10.6 Organizations providing guidance and/or assessments for socially responsible corporate action

- Global Reporting Initiative: https://www.globalreporting.org

- The International Organization for Standardization, ISO 26000 – Social Responsibility: http://www.iso.org/iso/home/standards/iso26000.htm

- Green Seal: http://www.greenseal.org

- B Impact Assessment: http://www.bimpactassessment.net

form across the country is called "B Lab." It provides an assessment process that leads to certification with a focus on the corporation's social and environmental impact. B Lab even offers a free self-assessment tool on its website making it easy for companies to self-measure and manage these impacts.[16] Several other organizations providing either guidance on operating a socially responsible entity or a means for certification, also exist. As shown in Box 10.6, each should be explored to find the one that is right for your business operations and mission.

In sum, through a benefits corporation a company is taking its resources from the private sector in order to create a public benefit. Whether through offering grants to solve social and environmental problems, providing job training, or deciding to source more from local suppliers, the beauty of this system is that the design of the mandate to consistently give back to the surrounding community is at the election of the corporation. It can therefore create the deliverables best suited for its immediate community and constituents, while simultaneously strengthening its brand image and recognition in the marketplace as a socially responsible company.

Key terms

accelerator	incubator	pledge
benefit corporation	limited liability	resident
C-Corporation	company	S-Corporation
crowdfunding	members	shareholders
defaults	minutes	smart fabrics
general public benefit	operating agreement	sole proprietor LLC

Discussion questions and exercises

1 Research an organization providing an assessment program for certification as a benefit corporation and prepare an overview of the requirements involved for obtaining the certification.

2 Create a crowdfunding campaign and (a) describe which platform you would choose and (2) why you consider it the best option to raise the money you are seeking.

3 Research wearable technologies and find three of them you think could improve your life. Explain how each would do so.

Notes

1. http://www.apple.com/apple-watch-hermes/ (viewed on January 8, 2017).
2. https://www.merriam-webster.com/dictionary/incubator (viewed on January 12, 2017).
3. This is not an all-inclusive list of every accelerator or incubator that exists. These were however, all in existence at the time of publication (viewed on July 9, 2017).
4. http://www.nyftlab.com/theprogram (viewed on January 12, 2017).
5. Resource Guide for Small Business, Small Business Administration, New York Edition (2016). https://www.sba.gov/sites/default/files/files/resourceguide_3135.pdf (viewed on January 19, 2017).

6. https://www.nytimes.com/2017/02/17/nyregion/bill-de-blasio-state-of-the-city-address.html?_r=0 (viewed on February 21, 2017).

7. https://www.kickstarter.com/about?ref=nav (viewed on January 22, 2017).

8. Each of the listed platforms were viewed and active as of January 22, 2017.

9. https://www.kickstarter.com/about?ref=nav (viewed on January 22, 2017).

10. https://www.kickstarter.com/help/faq/kickstarter+basics?ref=footer   (viewed   on January 22, 2017).

11. Ibid.

12. Article 17 of the New York State Business Corporation Law (BCL).

13. BCL §1702(b).

14. https://www.dos.ny.gov/corps/benefit_corporation_formation.html (viewed on January 22, 2017).

15. BCL §1702(e).

16. http://www.bimpactassessment.net (viewed on January 22, 2017).

Glossary

Administrative agency A governmental body with the authority to implement and administer particular legislation.

Air waybill The contract of carriage for shipments transported by air.

All or virtually all made in the US This country of origin standard requires that all significant parts and processing that go into a product must be of US origin and contain either none, or merely a negligible amount of, foreign content. When found, an unqualified US origin claim such as "Made in America" may be used.

Benefit corporation A corporation which is obligated to not only comply with general corporate requirements, but is also formed for the purpose of creating a general public benefit.

Bill of lading The contract of carriage for a vessel shipment which is a document of title acknowledging the receipt of goods by a carrier or by the shipper's agent.

Bond A monetary pledge to abide by US Customs laws.

Booking number The reservation number assigned by a carrier to hold space on the vessel for cargo being exported, and is required to be reported in AES Direct.

Buyer The principal party in the export transaction that purchases the commodities for delivery to the ultimate consignee.

Care label This label states what regular care is needed for the ordinary use of a product, which for wearing apparel specifically means having either a washing or dry-cleaning instruction.

C-Corporation A corporation eligible for tax treatment under Subchapter C of the US tax code.

Chargeback A fee for the late delivery, or a failure to deliver, conforming goods.

Children's products Those products designed or intended primarily for children twelve years of age or younger.

Children's sleepwear Any product of wearing apparel, either up to and including size 6X, or sized 7 through 14, including nightgowns, pajamas, or similar and related items, such as robes, which are intended to be worn primarily for sleeping or activities related to sleeping, except diapers and underwear, infant garments, and tight fitting garments.

Children's tracking label rule Requires information be placed on a children's product to identify its source and other production information.

Claim A notice filed with an insurance company seeking payment for the value of lost, stolen or damaged cargo.

Class A category of fabrics or related materials having general constructional or finished characteristics, and which are covered by a description generally recognized in the trade.

Commerce All commerce which may lawfully be regulated by Congress.

Component part Any part of a consumer product, including a children's product, that either must, or may, be tested separately from a finished consumer product in order to assess its ability to comply with a specific regulation enforced by CPSC.

Conscious consumer One who makes purchasing decisions based on factors that extend beyond the mere aesthetic or functionality of the article, which can include a company's business practices.

Consolidated containers Where a shipping container holds the packages of multiple shippers.

Continuing guaranty A guaranty issued which is valid for an initial three years, that must be renewed every three years thereafter, or at any such time as there is a change in the legal business status of the company filing the guaranty.

Contract of carriage A contract for the transport of freight.

Copyright A form of intellectual property that protects an original work of authorship fixed in any tangible medium of expression from which such work can be either directly perceived, reproduced, or otherwise communicated, or done so with the aid of a machine or device.

Counterfeit goods Those intending to be passed off as the original article itself.

Counterfeit mark A spurious designation which is identical with, or substantially indistinguishable from, a registered mark.

Counterfeit trademark This term, as defined by US Customs, means a spurious mark identical with, or substantially indistinguishable from, a federally registered trademark.

Country of destination The country where the goods are to be consumed, further processed, stored, or manufactured.

Country of origin The country of manufacture, production or growth of any article of foreign origin entering the US.

Country of origin of an apparel or textile product The country, territory, or insular possession in which a good originates, or of which a good is the growth, product, or manufacture.

Crocking The tendency of dye to rub off of a fabric due to dyeing methods, penetration or post-dyeing treatments.

Crowdfunding campaign Sourcing funds through several people which do not have to be repaid within a particular time frame.

Customs agency The government agency responsible for regulating the lawful entry of foreign goods through their own domestic borders.

Customs broker A party licensed by US Customs who files the entry documents on behalf of the importer of record pursuant to a fully executed power of attorney.

Customs duties A product specific tax assessed on imported merchandise and payable to the government at the time of importation.

Date of export The date when goods are scheduled to leave the port of export on the exporting carrier that is taking the goods out of the US.

Deductible An amount that must be paid in advance by an insured prior to the remainder of a claim being paid by an insurance company.

Default In the context of a loan is where the borrower does not repay the loan.

Defendant The party against whom plaintiff's claims are made.

Design patent protection The type of patent sought to protect the ornamental features of a useful article and typically covers the shape of a product and its surface ornamentation.

Domestic export Such goods that are grown, produced, or manufactured in the US, along with commodities of foreign origin that have been changed in the US from the form in which they were imported.

Drawstring A non-retractable cord, ribbon, or tape of any material to pull together parts of upper outerwear to provide for closure.

Endangered species An animal or plant listed by regulation as being in danger of extinction throughout all or a significant portion of its range.

Endorsement Any advertising message for which consumers are likely to believe is reflective of the opinion, finding, experience, or belief of the endorser.

Endorser An organization, consumer, expert, or celebrity providing an endorsement.

Enhancement Defined in the export regulations to mean a change or modification to a good which increases its value or improves its condition.

Entry The term for describing both the act of getting merchandise cleared through US Customs (verb) as well as the paper work involved in doing so (noun).

Expert An individual, group, or institution possessing, as a result of experience, study, or training, knowledge of a particular subject, which knowledge is superior to what ordinary individuals generally acquire.

Export Any item sent or transported from the US to a foreign destination.

Exporter Anyone engaged in selling goods internationally.

Fabric Any material that is woven, knitted, felted, or otherwise produced from, or in combination with, any natural or synthetic fiber, film, or substitute thereof.

Fair Trade A concept in which the conditions that facilitate international trade are equitable to all players engaged in the transaction with an emphasis on securing and maintaining (1) the sustainable development of producers supplying goods and (2) the rights, whether economic, social, cultural or otherwise, of those individuals actually providing the labor.

Fashion compliance Abiding by the laws that regulate a business in the fashion industry.

Fashion law As used in this book, is the compilation of several bodies of law that collectively regulate such sales of fashion merchandise and those entities engaged in facilitating this commercial activity.

Federal Maritime Commission (FMC) The US government agency that has regulatory oversight of vessels transiting the ports of the US.

Filer The party completing the AES form.

Filing (of customs entry) This includes the deposit of estimated duties and any accompanying entry summary documentation or data required for customs to assess duties, collect statistics, and determine a shipment's legality in relation to other laws which is a precondition to the release of imported merchandise from CBP custody.

Flammability Those characteristics of a material that pertain to its relative ease of ignition and relative ability to sustain combustion.

Foreign principal party in interest The non-US person or entity which has purchased the goods for export or is to whom final delivery or end-use of the goods will be made.

Forwarding agent The person in the US authorized by the principal party in interest to facilitate the movement of the cargo from the US to the foreign destination and/or to prepare and file the required documentation.

Freedom to operate The process of determining whether patent protection on a product would lead to infringement of another party's patent.

Freight forwarder Broadly defined within the international trade community as a person engaged in the business of assembling, collecting, consolidating, shipping and distributing less than a carload or less than a truckload of freight and who acts as an agent in the transshipping of freight to or from foreign countries.

Freight forwarder services Refers to the dispatching of shipments on behalf of others in order to facilitate the transportation by a common carrier.

General certificate of conformity A document which certifies a product's compliance with all rules and regulations under the Consumer Product Safety Act (CPSA).

General public benefit A material positive impact on society and the environment, taken as a whole and assessed against a third party standard.

Guarantor The person certifying the guaranty.

Harmonized System (HS) The nomenclature for international goods that enables products to be identified by the same classification code all over the world.

Household textile articles A textile good of a type customarily used in a household regardless of where in fact it is used such as wearing apparel, draperies, floor coverings, furnishings, beddings, costumes and accessories.

Importer of record The owner or purchaser of cargo.

Incoterms A series of standardized shipping terms defined by the International Chamber of Commerce that apportions the costs and liabilities of international shipping between buyers and sellers.

Incubator An organization or place that aids the development of new business ventures especially by providing low-cost commercial space, management assistance, or shared services.

Infant garment A garment that is sized for nine months or younger, or is a one-piece garment which does not exceed 64.8 centimeters (25.75 inches) in length, or if a two-piece garment, has no piece exceeding 40 centimeters (15.75 inches) in length.

Infringing goods Merchandise using the intellectual property of another without authorization to do so.

Insured The party purchasing the insurance policy.

Intellectual property Refers to creations of the mind that are creative works or ideas embodied in a shareable form which can enable others to re-create, emulate, or manufacture them.

Intent-to-use basis The status of filing for a trademark or service mark where an applicant has a bonafide intention to use such mark on their goods or services they are or are planning to sell.

Interlinings or interlining fabrics Any fabric or fibers incorporated into an article of wearing apparel as a layer between an outer shell and an inner lining.

Intermediate consignee The person or entity in the foreign country who acts as an agent for the principal party in interest with the purpose of effecting delivery of items to the ultimate consignee.

Knock off A virtual replica of the original article.

Label A stamp, tag, label, or other means of identification affixed securely and containing all of the regulatory mandated information in a legible, conspicuous and non-deceptive format, in the English language to a textile, wool or fur product.

Lead-containing paint Any paint or other similar surface coating material containing lead or lead compounds where the lead content exceeds 0.009 percent by weight of the total nonvolatile content of the paint, or the weight of the dried paint film.

License An authorization by a licensor for a licensee to use something that belongs to the licensor for a certain period of time, such as its intellectual property.

Licensee The party leasing the use of another's intellectual property.

Licensing The sale of a license authorizing another to use something, such as one's intellectual property.

Licensor The entity which owns the intellectual property to be licensed.

Liquidation The final computation of duties on an entry.

Logistics The process of planning, implementing and controlling the flow of personnel, materials and information from the point of origin to the point of destination, at the required time, and in the desired condition.

Material In the context of advertising, it means where a representation made about a product is likely to affect consumers' choices or conduct regarding it.

Material facts In the context of advertising, are those facts that are important to consumer's choices or conduct regarding a product.

Members Owners of a limited liability corporation.

Minutes The recordation of notes taken at a meeting of corporate officers, directors or shareholders.

Misbranding A broad range of labeling errors, including those not simply improperly labeled, stamped, tagged or marked, but also where the text of any Required Information is minimized, rendered obscure or inconspicuous, or is placed in a way likely to be unnoticed or unseen by purchasers when the product is offered or displayed for sale, or sold to purchasers.

Misleading door opener When the first contact between a seller and buyer occurs through a deceptive practice.

Mode of transportation The method by which goods are exported from the US and includes vessel, air, truck, rail, mail or other methods of transport.

Native advertisement or advertising Where a product's marketing is incorporated into what appears to be a news article, or is such the case where a paid influencer promotes a product to its fan base of followers as if they were promoting it without being paid to do so.

Net impression Evaluates whether an advertisement's overall format would be misleading rather than looking at it in isolation.

Non-vessel-operating common carrier (NVOCC) A common carrier which does not operate the vessels by which the ocean transportation is provided, and is a shipper in its relationship with an ocean common carrier.

Ocean freight forwarder A person who dispatches shipments from the US via a common carrier, books or otherwise arranges space for those shipments on behalf of shippers, and may collect, consolidate, ship and distribute less than container loads of freight. It may also process the documentation or perform related activities incident to those shipments.

Omni-channel retailing Retailers that operate both stores and websites and encourage shopping across channels so that purchasers will shop both online and in stores.

Ocean transportation intermediary (OTI) Either a non-vessel-operating-common-carrier which is commonly referred to as an "NVOCC" or an "ocean freight forwarder."

Operating agreement An agreement that establishes how an LLC will operate.

Ornamentation Any fibers or yarns imparting a visibly discernible pattern or design to a yarn or fabric.

Paint and other similar surface-coating materials Fluid, semi-fluid, or other materials which change to a solid film when a thin layer is applied to a metal, paper, leather, cloth, plastic, or other surface.

Plain surface textile fabric Any textile fabric which does not have an intentionally raised fiber or yarn surface such as a pile, nap, or tuft, but does include those fabrics that have fancy woven, knitted or flock-printed surfaces.

Plaintiff The party that has started a lawsuit.

Pledge Money supporting a crowdfunding campaign.

Port of export Either the CBP seaport or airport where the goods are loaded on to the aircraft or vessel that is taking the cargo out of the US, or the CBP port where exports by overland transportation cross the US border into Canada or Mexico.

Port of unlading The place where the cargo will be removed from the airplane, vessel, or other mode of transport.

Premium The cost of an insurance policy.

Price actually paid or payable The total payment (whether direct or indirect, and exclusive of any costs, charges, or expenses incurred for transportation, insurance, and related services incident to the international shipment of the merchandise from the country of exportation to the place of importation in the US) made, or to be made, for imported merchandise by the buyer to, or for the benefit of, the seller.

Principal parties in interest Those persons in a transaction that receive the primary benefit, monetary or otherwise, from the transaction.

Program of reasonable and representative tests At least one test which is the subject of an initial guaranty, with results demonstrating conformance with the Flammability Standard performed either within or outside of the territories of the US.

Protest A challenge brought against a US Customs decision.

Qualified Made in USA claim This statement indicates the amount, extent, or type of a product's domestic processing or content, and indicates that the product is not entirely of US domestic origin.

Qualified marketing claim Where there is a caveat that accompanies a blanket marketing statement made about a product in order to specify to what extent such statement is truthful.

Rail waybill The freight document that indicates goods have been received for shipment by rail.

Raised surface textile fabrics Fabrics with an intentionally raised fiber or yarn surface, such as velvet or other pile fabrics.

Recycled content Includes used, reconditioned and re-manufactured components, as well as recycled raw materials.

Recycled wool Either (1) the resulting fiber when wool has been woven or felted into a wool product which, without ever having been utilized in any way by the ultimate consumer, subsequently has been made into a fibrous state, or (2) the resulting fiber when wool or reprocessed wool has been spun, woven, knitted, or felted into a wool product which, after having been used in any way by the ultimate consumer is subsequently made into a fibrous state.

Regulations What statutes are converted into which allow a federal government agency, to implement the laws drafted by Congress.

Remnants Portions of fabric severed from their bolts or rolls where the fiber content of such piece of fabric may be known or unknown.

Repurposing Using goods that would otherwise be discarded towards another useful purpose.

Required Information All of the information required to be contained in a label under the regulations for textile, wool and fur products.

Reshoring Efforts to bring back manufacturing to the US.

Resident Indicates the state in which a US corporation is physically located in.

Restricted gray market articles Foreign-made articles bearing a genuine trademark or trade name identical with or substantially indistinguishable from one owned and recorded by a citizen of the United States or a corporation or association created or organized within the United States and imported without the authorization of the US owner.

Schedule B number A 10-digit commodity classification number for exports administered by the US Census Bureau and is the common name for the "Statistical Classification of Domestic and Foreign Commodities Exported from the United States."

Secondary meaning A concept under trademark law which is when in the minds of the public, the primary significance of a product feature is to identify the source of the product rather than the product itself.

S-Corporation A corporation eligible for tax treatment under Subchapter S of the US tax code.

Seize The act by US Customs of confiscating imported merchandise.

Seller The principal party in an export transaction, who is usually the manufacturer, producer, wholesaler, or distributor of the goods, and who receives the monetary benefit or other consideration for the exported goods.

Separable A concept under copyright law for which copyright protection is only extended to such design elements of clothing which are physically or conceptually separate from the garment itself.

Separate guaranty An individual guaranty.

Service mark Any word, name, symbol, or device, or any combination thereof either used by a person, or for which a person has a bona fide intention to use in commerce such word, name, etc. to identify and distinguish the services of one person or entity from the services of others and to indicate the source of the services.

Shareholders The owners of a corporation.

Shipper May have several identities, including that of a cargo owner, the person for whose account the ocean transportation is provided or to whom delivery is to be made, or an NVOCC that accepts responsibility for payment of all applicable charges.

Shipping documents Records including, but not limited to, the commercial invoice, export shipping instructions, a packing list, and the bill of lading or air waybill.

Shipment reference number A unique identification number assigned to the shipment by the filer for reference purposes.

Small batch manufacturer One who has manufactured no more than 7,500 units of the same product and whose total gross revenues of all consumer products from the prior calendar year is $1,086,627 or less.

Smart fabrics Fabrics which offer a specific functionality due to the incorporation of, e.g., certain chemicals into the fabrics.

Sole proprietor LLC A limited liability corporation comprised of only one member.

Statutory factors Factors CPSC is mandated to follow for making a penalty determination.

Substantial product hazards Product defects that create a substantial risk of injury for reasons such as the severity of the risk, or the pattern of defect.

Substantial transformation This occurs when an article emerges from a process with a new name, character or use which is different from that possessed by the article prior to the processing, and will not merely result from a minor manufacturing or combining process that leaves the identity of the article intact.

Supply chain sustainability The management of environmental, social and economic impacts and the encouragement of good governance practices, throughout the lifecycles of goods and services.

Tariff (FMC related) The price set by a carrier for the transport of goods and includes the actual rates, charges, classifications, rules, regulations and practices of a common carrier or a group of related ones.

Tariff classification number The classification code that is recognized globally under the HS as this product.

Textile fiber products Any fiber or yarn, in either a finished or unfinished state, that is used or intended for use in a household textile article and is not a product containing wool.

Textile or apparel product (US Customs) Any good classifiable in Chapters 50 through 63 of the HTSUS.

Third party conformity assessment body A CPSC certified test lab.

Title Legal ownership.

Traceable Where all testing parties are identifiable, including their name and address, which could be a manufacturer, supplier, or test lab.

Trade dress The image and overall appearance or presentation of a product.

Trademark Any word, name, symbol, design, or any combination thereof, used in commerce to identify and distinguish the goods of one manufacturer or seller from those of another and to indicate the source of the goods – even if the source is unknown.

Transaction value The "price actually paid or payable" for merchandise when sold for exportation to the US, plus the amounts for other items if not included in the seller's price.

Trimmings Textile fibers of a minimal quantity of the surface area of the wearing apparel such as tape, gussets, cuffs, braids, labels, findings, and other decorative trim.

Trucker's bill of lading A freight document that indicates goods have been received for shipment by truck.

Ultimate consignee The person, party, or designee that is located abroad and actually receives the exported shipment.

Ultimate purchaser The last person in the US who will receive the article in the form in which it was imported.

Uncovered or exposed part That part of an article of wearing apparel that might be susceptible to a flame or other means of ignition when worn under normal use, as well as linings with exposed areas.

Unqualified marketing claim Where only a blanket statement is made about a product.

Upcycling A process where post-consumer textiles are made into new apparel or accessories.

Use in commerce The bona fide use of a mark in the ordinary course of trade.

US Customs and Border Protection (CBP) The US government agency that regulates American customs procedures and tariff laws.

US principal party in interest (USPPI) The person or legal entity in the US that receives the primary benefit, monetary or otherwise, from the export transaction.

Utility patent protection The type of patent protection sought to protect the structure and function of an invention which is novel, useful and non-obvious.

Wearing apparel any costume, article of clothing, or covering for any part of the body worn or intended to be worn by individuals (as defined under the Textile Fiber Products Identification Act).

Wholly assembled A concept under customs law about a product where at least two components of it preexisted in essentially the same condition as found in the finished good, yet were combined to form the finished good in a single country, territory, or insular possession.

Wool The fiber from the fleece of the sheep or lamb, the hair of the Angora or Cashmere goat, or the specialty fibers from the hair of the camel, alpaca, llama and vicuna.

Wool products Any product, or portion of a product, which contains or in any way is represented as containing wool or represented as containing recycled wool.

Work for hire A copyrightable work produced either by an employee within the scope of employment or by an independent contractor under a written agreement.

Index

Entries in **bold** denote figures